D1114818

Horizontal Divestiture and the Petroleum Industry

Horizontal Divestiture and the Petroleum Industry

Jesse W. Markham
Graduate School of Business Administration
Harvard University

Anthony P. Hourihan
Graduate School of Business Administration
Harvard University

Francis L. Sterling
Management Analysis Center, Inc.

Ballinger Publishing Company • Cambridge, Massachusetts
A Subsidiary of J.B. Lippincott Company

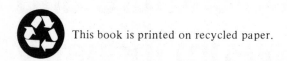 This book is printed on recycled paper.

Library of Congress Cataloging in Publication Data

Markham, Jesse William, 1916-
   Horizontal divestiture and the petroleum industry.

   1. Petroleum industry and trade—United States. 2. Corporate divesti-
ture—United States. I. Hourihan, Anthony P., joint author. II. Sterling,
Francis L., joint author. III. Title.
HD9566.M37   338.2'7'2820973   77-3350
ISBN 0-88410-471-0

Copyright © 1977 by Ballinger Publishing Company. All rights reserved.
No part of this publication may be reproduced, stored in a retrieval
system, or transmitted in any form or by any means, electronic mechanical
photocopy, recording or otherwise, without the prior written consent of
the publisher.

International Standard Book Number: 0-88410-471-0

Library of Congress Catalog Card Number: 77-3350

Printed in the United States of America

HD
9566
M37

To: Penelope, Laura, and Molly

16.6.8

Midwest

8cpo14

432345

Contents

List of Figures   xi

List of Tables   xiii

Preface   xvii

Introduction   xxi

Chapter One
Concentration Levels and Market Power   1

Chapter Two
Concentration in the Energy Industry   7

Chapter Three
Assessment of Oil Company Behavior in
Relation to Development of Alternative
Energy Resources   27

The Research Data Base   28
Alternative Energy Source Price Competition   30

Utility Fuel Substitutability   33
Economic Feasibility   36
Physical Feasibility   40
Conclusion   45
The Financing of Non-Petroleum Energy Resource
Development   46
Capital Requirements for Non-Petroleum
Energy Resource Recovery   46
Projected Availability of Capital Funds   53
Sources of Capital Funds   57
Energy Resource Research and Development   65
Magnitude of R&D   69
Output of R&D   70
Commercialization/Licensing   75
Technology: Transfer and Synergy   76
R&D Trends   79
Development Examples   81
Conclusion   85

Chapter Four
The Pro-Competitive Structural Aspects
of Horizontal Diversification   89

Asymmetry Defined   90
Asymmetry in the Petroleum Industry   91
Conclusion   93

Chapter Five
Conclusions   97

There is No Need for Structural Remedies   97
Withholding-of-Production Would Be Irrational   98
Conclusion   101

Appendix A
Non-Petroleum Energy Patents and Patent
Holders   107

Appendix B
Energy Activities of Petroleum Companies
by Size Group   115

Appendix C
Continental Oil Company: Research and
Engineering Interactions   119

Appendix D
The Status of Synthetic Fuel Projects   123

Index   151

About the Authors   155

List of Figures

3-1   Illustration of Corporate Net External Funds
Required as Percent of Net Savings in the
Household Sector   56

3-2   Trend of Specific Area Expenditures as
Percent Total of R&D Budget, 1975-1980   80

3-3   Projected Trend of Specific Area
Expenditures as Percent of Total R&D
Budget 1975-1980   82

5-1   Energy Resources Reserves and Consumption
Pattern   99

5-2   Demand/Supply Projections for All Forms of
Energy to 1985   105

List of Tables

2-1   Concentration Ratios Using Selected
       Definitions of the Energy Industry, Based
       on Production in BTU Equivalents—1974   11

2-2   Concentration Ratios for Selected
       Definitions of the Energy Industry, Based
       on Privately Controlled Reserves Expressed
       in BTU Equivalents—1975   12

2-3   U.S. Net Crude Oil, Condensate and Natural
       Gas Liquids Production Concentration
       Ratios 1955, 1960, 1965, 1970, 1974   13

2-4   U.S. Net Natural Gas Production Concentration
       Ratios—1955, 1960, 1965, 1970, 1974   13

2-5   U.S. Bituminous Coal and Lignite Production
       Concentration Ratios—1955, 1960, 1965
       1970, 1974   14

2-6   U.S. Uranium Oxide Concentrate Production
       Concentration Ratios—1955, 1960, 1965,
       1970, 1975   15

2-7   The Twenty Top Domestic Energy Producers
       for Selected Energy Industry Definitions—
       1974   18

2-8   The Twenty Top Domestic Energy Reserve
       Holders for Selected Energy Industry
       Definitions—1975   19

2-9   Known Federally and Corporate Controlled
       Energy Reserves—1975   21

2-10   Concentration Ratios for Selected
            Definitions of the Energy Industry, Based
            on Privately and Publicly Controlled
            Reserves Expressed in BTU Equivalents—1975   22
3-1   Percent Utilization of Primary Fuels by
            Consumption Sector—1970   31
3-2   Annual Industrial and Total Consumption of
            Bituminous Coal—1935-1975   32
3-3   Average Monthly Delivered Cost—Electric
            Utility Fuel Oil and Coal—April, 1973-
            October, 1975   34
3-4   Delivered Cost of Eastern and Western Coals
            Western Pennsylvania Utility—1975   40
3-5   Approximate Cost Components for Western
            Coal and Persian Gulf Crude Oil   41
3-6   U.S. Refined Product Sales of Fourteen
            Selected Major Refiners—1975   42
3-7   Consolidation Coal Sales and End Use—1965-
            1973   43
3-8   Gulf Oil Company—U.S. and Foreign Refined
            Products Sales—1975   45
3-9   Historic and Projected Energy Demand Growth
            by Sector   47
3-10   Projected U.S. Annual Energy Requirements
            and Contribution by Energy Sector   48
3-11   Energy Demand by Sector—1985   49
3-12   Estimated Per Unit Capital Requirements for
            Recovery of Selected Energy Resources   50
3-13   Case 1—Energy Sources   51
3-14   Case 1—Capital Investment Requirements   51
3-15   Case 2—Capital Investment Requirements   52
3-16   Case 3—Capital Investment Requirements   53
3-17   Estimated Capital Requirements for Recovery
            of Selected Energy Resources, 1975-1984   54
3-18   Investor-Owned Electric Utility: 1975-1985
            External Financing Including Pollution
            Control   60
3-19   Capital Expenditures by Selected Major
            Petroleum Companies—1975   62
3-20   1974 Debt-to-Equity Ratio for Selected
            Major Industries   63
3-21   Worldwide Return on Equity of Petroleum
            Companies 1965-1974   64

3-22	1974 Fixed-to-Total Assets Ratios for Selected Major Industries	65
3-23	The Importance of the Petroleum and Electric Utility Industries in Total Output of the Economy, Aggregate Plant and Equipment Expenditures, and External Capital Markets—1970	66
3-24	New Plant and Equipment Expenditures for Oil, Gas and Investor Owned Utility Industries	67
3-25	Capital Expenditures	68
3-26	Total Industrial R&D Expenditures for Energy by Industry—1972-1974	69
3-27	Energy R&D Expenditures and Sales Revenues of 23 Major Oil Companies	71
3-28	Petroleum Company Patents and Revenues	72
3-29	Coal Conversion Patents by Type of Company, 1964-1975	73
3-30	Oil Shale Patents by Type of Company, 1964-1975	74
3-31	Oil Shale Patent Holders Participants in Commercial or Demonstration Projects (as of March, 1976)	75
3-32	Licensing Revenues	76
4-1	Comparison of Amerada Hess with Cities Service Selected North American Operations, 1975	92
4-2	Selected Operating Statistics, 1975	93
4-3	Selected Statistics, 1975	94
5-1	U.S. Consumption of Energy Resources by Major Sources and Consuming Sectors, 1974 Preliminary and Projected to the Year 2000	102
5-2	Forecasts of Domestic Liquid-Fuel Supply/Demand in 1985	104
5-3	Average Gulf Coast Cargo Prices, 1970-1974	106
A-1	Coal Conversion Patents Summary Sheet	108
A-2	Petroleum Companies Summary Sheet: Patents Relating to Coal Conversion	108
A-3	Coal Conversion Patents	109
A-4	Oil Shale Patents Summary Sheet	111
A-5	Patents Relating to Oil Shale Processing: Petroleum Companies Summary Sheet	111
A-6	Oil Shale Processing Patents	112
B-1	Comparison of U.S. Petroleum, Coal, Uranium	

Concentrate, and Geothermal Energy
Production by Top Eight Ranked Domestic
Petroleum Producers, 1974   116

B-2   Comparison of U.S. Petroleum, Coal, Uranium
Concentrate, and Geothermal Energy
Production by Domestic Petroleum Producers
Ranked 9-20, 1974   117

B-3   Comparison of U.S. Petroleum, Coal, Uranium
Concentrate, and Geothermal Energy
Production by Small Domestic Petroleum
Producers, 1974   118

Preface

The Middle East "October War" of 1973 set in motion a train of events that led swiftly to intense preoccupation— on both the policy and political fronts—with the structure of the U.S. domestic oil industry. A few months before the OPEC imposed its oil embargo on the United States, with its attendant increased gasoline prices, long waiting lines, and Sunday closing of service stations, the Federal Trade Commission issued its complaint against the eight largest oil companies (*Federal Trade Commission v. Exxon et al.*), contemplating both their horizontal and vertical divestiture. By the end of 1975, Senators Hart, Bayh, Abourezk, Tunney, and Packwood had introduced a bill in the Senate (S.2387) seeking vertical divestiture of the large oil companies, which was quickly followed by the introduction of the Interfuel Competition Act (S.489), seeking horizontal divestiture of these same companies, including divestiture of their operations in non-oil energy sources. In the 95th Congress some 20 bills have been introduced calling for divestiture.

By 1976 "divestiture" had become as much a political slogan as an antitrust objective, taking on the high emotion of the "free silver" issue of an earlier era. The Democratic Party made it a plank in their platform, and it served as the one rallying point for the dozen or so candidates seeking the Democratic Party's 1976 presidential nomination. Spot TV political advertisements proclaiming each candidate's support of divestiture of the oil companies were projected on the viewing audience with the frequency of detergent and toothpaste ads—reaching a somewhat confusing level of specificity with candidate Fred Harris's promise to break up the eighteen (*sic*) oil monopolies.

Yet the singleminded preoccupation with divestiture was fraught with ambiguities. At about the same time the FTC initiated its case, the Treasury Department released a study contending that the oil industry was not highly concentrated according to the FTC's own findings and, furthermore, the FTC data overstated the actual level of concentration. Senator Philip Hart, in his luncheon speech at the Airlie House Conference on Concentration on March 2, 1974, observed with his characteristic candidness that, by conventional standards, the oil industry was not among our most highly concentrated industries. Walter Measday, staff economist for the Senate Committee on the Judiciary, Subcommittee on Antitrust and Monopoly, in his address to the Stanford University Conference on Divestiture in September 1976, stated that "available statistics provide a surface appearance of moderate concentration . . . far less, for example, than we can find in a number of other industries. . . . ."

It was inevitable that at some time in these proceedings the oil industry itself would raise such questions as: Just how concentrated are we?, and "On what factual evidence is our industry being singled out for divestiture by the highly unusual means of industry-specific legislation?" In the early winter of 1976 the American Petroleum Institute engaged Management Analysis Center, Incorporated, of Cambridge, Massachusetts, to assemble and analyze all the available facts pertaining to these questions.

Not surprisingly, our analysis reaches conclusions broadly consistent with those of others who have examined comparable data before—the domestic oil industry, under any of several reasonable definitions of the industry, is not among our more highly concentrated industries; in fact, it is no more concentrated than the average for all manufacturing and mining industries generally. However, it became apparent early in our analysis that the issues raised by the proposed legislation contemplating divestiture involved more than the simple compilation of conventional concentration ratios.

Petroleum companies are in the process of becoming energy companies—extending their investment and R&D into non-oil sources of energy. The proposed Interfuel Competition Act (S.489) would not only arrest but reverse the process. Since a plausible case can be made that the growth of multi-energy companies, for several reasons, will enhance competition in the energy industry generally and in its component subsectors (gas, oil, coal, uranium, and so on), the enactment of the proposed bill might well have the effect of defeating its alleged purposes. Of equal importance, an objective of our national energy policy—Project Independence—is to liberate the nation's economy from the vagaries of imported oil availability by developing our non-oil energy resources. Again, the proposed Inter-fuel Competition Act would appear to be at odds with this objective. Since the petroleum companies are becoming the prime movers in developing new energy technologies and non-oil energy sources, it is not at all clear who will replace them should they be dislodged.

While in our view the extensive factual analysis leads to these conclusions, we consider the essential contribution of this book to be the facts themselves. In this connection we owe a debt of gratitude to those who made them available, and to those who helped assemble them. Particularly, we are indebted to the twenty-three large- and medium-sized petroleum (energy) companies, who cooperated with us in our field investigations and who responded to our detailed data requests; to the American Petroleum Institute, who served as a ready reference library on government documents and who made available to us their computerized patent data bank; to Irvin C. Bupp, Jr. of the Harvard Business School; and to Linda Kanner and Lee Gladden of the Management Analysis Center staff. We, of course, are responsible for any errors or omissions, and for the analyses and conclusions.

Jesse W. Markham
Anthony P. Hourihan
Francis L. Sterling

Introduction

The critical intermediate-term energy problem confronting the United States, a problem confronting all industrialized nations, is the growing gap between the consumption and domestic production of oil and gas. These two forms of energy account for approximately 75 percent of our annual energy consumption, and the upward trend in their consumption relative to domestic production is making us increasingly reliant on imports of these fuels. Within the memory of most who will read this book the United States was a net oil exporter, and less than two decades ago we pursued a public policy of restricting imports for the ostensible purpose of maintaining our self-sufficiency in oil—an early and simplistic version of Project Independence. By 1971, imports from the Middle East and Africa reached 24.5 percent of domestic consumption, the preliminary figures for 1976 place total imports at 40 percent, and it is estimated that by 1980 they will be 50 percent. Meanwhile, since 1968 the United States has been consuming natural gas at twice the rate it has been discovering it.

If it could be assumed that international trade in oil were free—governed by the competitive forces of supply and demand—we would not face in the twentieth century an energy problem any more than it could be said that we face a cocoa, banana, or coffee problem. The estimated proven oil reserves of the Middle East and Asia alone amount to 348 billion barrels. At their current rate of production of 8.6 billion barrels per year, these reserves alone would supply the producing countries and their present customers, including the United States, well into the twenty-first century, leaving the rest of the world's reserves to supply the annual growth in consumption. Moreover, the United States has vast reserves of coal amounting to three times the energy contained in the Middle East's total oil reserves. Since the turn of the century, however, consumption patterns have shifted in the United States from where coal, once supplying 90 percent of our energy needs, now supplies only 18 percent. Meanwhile, nuclear plants have come on stream, liquefaction and gasification of coal techniques are evolving, and solar, thermal, and fusion technologies are in their infancy.

It is obvious, therefore, that the future energy economy of the United States will be significantly determined by two closely related factors: (1) technology—the development of new energy sources, new techniques for using our vast coal reserves, and new and more efficient means of oil and gas exploration and recovery; and (2) the extent to which the United States, as a matter of policy, seeks to reduce its dependency on oil and gas imports—the seriousness and effectiveness with which we pursue Project Independence.

The importance of the latter consideration is dealt with at some length in Chapter Three of this book. It is clear from all available data that the cost of a serious drive to develop new energy sources will be immense. The price tag of former Vice President Rockefeller's proposed energy development corporation has been estimated at $100 billion. Estimates for a concentrated and comprehensive 10-year drive to develop new technologies through research and development and creation of the requisite capital have been variously estimated at $597 billion (National Academy of Engineering), $628 billion (National Petroleum Council), and $700 billion (Hollander, Federal Reserve Board). This amounts to an annual average expenditure over the next 10 years of from $60 billion to $70 billion. Our own estimates, confined to development of the reasonably feasible energy sources of coal, synthetic fuels, and nuclear power, show that between 1976 and 1990, under three sets of assumptions, capital requirements will amount to from $88.8 billion to $212.8 billion.

⌊Clearly, then, our energy economy is in for substantial change—a process that is already underway. The prime movers in this change are those companies we have historically been describing as the major oil companies.⌋ Gradually, but quite perceptibly from the data, they are evolving into total energy companies. This metamorphosis is evident from the changing composition of their energy output, their capital expenditures, and their past and projected research and development (R&D) budgets. For example, five petroleum companies are now among the top twenty producers of coal, and three are among the largest fifteen producers of nuclear fuel. In 1975 nineteen major petroleum companies accounted for $1.2 billion of investment in nonpetroleum resources. Between 1971 and 1975 twenty-three petroleum companies increased their R&D outlays on nonpetroleum technology from $23.1 million to $120.9 million, and the share of their total R&D going to nonpetroleum energy technology increased from 8.6 to 23.7 percent.

Not only is the entry of petroleum companies into non-oil energy industries consistent with the objective of our national energy policy—the accelerated development of non-oil energy—it reflects the rational reallocative forces of the marketplace in three distinct ways: (1) the limits on oil reserves at home and the nationalization of those in which they held an equity position abroad have given oil companies a strong incentive to turn to other energy sources—they already have a large investment in managerial expertise and capital involved in the production and marketing of energy; (2) much of the technology of oil exploration, recovery, and refining is economically transferable to non-oil energy sources; and (3) oil companies, by any standard, are large and experienced in making extensive long-term investments that have prospective long-term payoffs.

The forces of the marketplace are reallocating our resources in precisely the direction contemplated by our national energy policy. For what possible cause, then, should Congress enact a supra-antitrust law requiring that this reallocation process be halted, indeed reversed? Since the proposed Interfuel Competition Act (S.489) requires not only that oil companies be prohibited from entering other energy industries, but also that they divest themselves of their present non-oil energy businesses, the relevant market for analysis is, by implication, the total energy market. Conventional economic wisdom holds that when the level of market concentration is very high, there is an enhanced probability that the few participating firms will so conduct themselves that the outcome in the marketplace will not differ substantially from that of monopoly. The mode of behavior of such concentrated industries has been captured in the descriptive terms "conscious parallelism," "conjectural interdependence," "oligopolistic rationalization," "competitive forebearance," or simply "tacit collusion." Since the monopoly behavior can be traced directly and uniquely to the industry's structure, the obvious remedy lies in a restructuring of the industry—dissolution of the few large firms that collectively exercise monopoly power over the marketplace.

While many empirical studies of industrial concentration have been highly instructive, they have fallen far short of providing a litmus test for establishing the threshold point at which independent competitive behavior among rival firms gives way to tacit cooperation. And although such studies have developed supportive factual evidence of the basic theoretical proposition that the *probability* of tacit cooperation—at least on the matter of price—increases as the four-firm concentration ratio approaches its upper limit of one hundred percent, the disparate patterns of competitive (cooperative) behavior even among highly concentrated industries has been found to be quite significant.

This qualification aside, there appears to be substantial agreement that the range of four-firm industrial concentration that should be of special public policy concern falls at 70 percent and above, and that concentration in the 50 to 70 percent range could, in certain circumstances, lead to patterns of conscious parallelism.

Concentration in the energy industry taken as a whole, and in all its subsector components except the uranium industry, fall considerably below these levels. For all energy, the four largest companies account for only 18.4 percent of total output; the largest eight for only 29.7 percent; and the largest twenty for 47.8 percent. In the petroleum industry, to which the Interfuel Competition Act is principally addressed, the largest four firms account for 26 percent, and the largest eight for 41.7 percent. The levels of concentration in natural gas and coal are even lower. In all three of these sectors of the energy industry, and in the energy industry as a whole, the level of concentration is considerably below the approximate average of 40 percent for all U.S. manufacturing.

In these circumstances the economic rationale for the intensive drive in Congress to radically restructure the energy industry by divesting oil companies of their non-oil energy businesses is, to say the least, obscure. This is especially so since the oil companies, by reallocating their capital and R&D resources to these businesses, is consistent with the government's overall energy policy. We therefore conclude that the Interfuel Competition Act has the potential for inflicting on the nation substantial economic losses with no visible offsetting economic gains in the form of more efficient resource allocation. The analysis that has led us to this conclusion is set forth in the chapters that follow.

Horizontal Divestiture and
the Petroleum Industry

 *Chapter One*

Concentration Levels and Market Power

Both economists and public policymakers have long been concerned with industries that are characterized as oligopolies on the basis of their high concentration ratios. This concern follows from a central tenet of economic theory: once a certain (high) level of concentration has been reached in an industry, the probability is great that member firms will recognize the mutual interdependence of their actions, and their behavior toward each other will become tacitly cooperative or competitively "forebearing," rather than competitive. It is therefore held that free and open competition, especially price competition, may become greatly reduced in the context of such "oligopolistic coordination." The form of oligopolistic behavior which, it is held, emanates from high levels of concentration may range from overt to tacit collusion; the term "conscious parallelism" is the term most frequently used by antitrust economists and lawyers in describing the likely outcome in highly concentrated industries.

Given the widespread acceptance, among both economists and public policymakers, of the relationship between high concentration ratios and an absence of competition, the central question that needs to be answered is: At what level of concentration does tacit collusion or conscious parallelism cease to be merely a possibility and become a probability? The conventional wisdom of this issue constitutes the remainder of this chapter. The ultimate objective is to see whether—given prevailing economic understanding of this issue and our structural analysis of the energy industry, regardless of how it is defined (see Chapter Two)—there is any reason why the level of concentration within the energy industry should be a matter of concern to either economists or public policymakers.

Before addressing the question, How much concentration is too much?, certain caveats are in order. First of all, it is unlikely that there is any single concentration ratio below which it can unambiguously be stated that active competition does exist, or above which competition is absent. It is equally unlikely that such a magic ratio, even if it existed, would be the same for all industries. Given these considerations it is essential to realize that what is being sought is not a single criterion but a range of figures, however derived, about which there is some degree of consensus among the experts. Secondly, it must be kept in mind that seller concentration is not the sole indicator of the existence or absence of competition in an industry. Even those economists who suggest that industries with concentration ratios above a certain level should be automatically restructured usually acknowledge that other variables—such as the existence of "excessive" profitability, or barriers-to-entry, or the absence of price competition—should be considered before such restructuring takes place. Perhaps one of the most succinct comments on this matter has been made by the noted antitrust lawyer and economist, Eugene Singer:

> Neither a single concentration index nor a combination of concentration indexes can be used as a direct measure of the degree of competition. Except in extreme cases where a few firms produce almost all of the output of an industry, the knowledge of the distribution of firms is insufficient, in and of itself, for the making of even a cursory judgement as to the nature of competition. Additional information is required, such as whether the industry is expanding or contracting, the extent of mergers, the rates of entry and exit of firms, the turnover in rank of the leading firms, research and development expenditures, the importance of substitute products, imports, exports, secondary markets and price flexibility. *The calculation of concentration ratios must therefore be perceived as the beginning and not the end of an antitrust analysis of market power.*[1]

Bearing these qualifications in mind we now turn to the central issue of how much market concentration is required for tacit collusion to take place. Fortunately, economists and antitrust experts have commented at length on this issue. Although there is no single test for resolving this matter, it would appear *that a four-firm concentration ratio of 50 percent* is a reasonable estimate of the point below which tacit collusion is difficult and unlikely. One of the pioneers in the economics of industrial organization, Joe Bain, has stated that in the highest concentration category, where more than

75 percent of industry output is supplied by the largest four sellers, firms would have a "maximum tendency to agree on a joint profit-maximizing price, and a minimum propensity to pursue independent and antagonistic policies."[2] In industries where the largest four sellers supply from 51 percent to 75 percent of industry output, Bain is of the opinion that "joint monopoly tendencies still appear probable" but that there is "an enhanced likelihood that these tendencies may be tempered or restrained by the independent, antagonistic policies of individual sellers."[3] Where the largest four sellers supply from 26 to 50 percent of industry output (a category into which the petroleum industry may fall depending on the industry definition used), Bain concludes that the mutually recognized interdependence of sellers may still be "strong enough that strictly independent action is counterbalanced by some tendency toward concerted action for maximum joint profits."[4] However, it should be pointed out that when Bain developed a classification of industries according to seller concentration, of the six "types" of market structures (ranked in descending order of concentration), he listed as Type IV—"low-moderate" concentration—those industries with roughly 35 to 50 percent of the market controlled by four firms, roughly 45 to 70 percent by eight, and with a large number of sellers in all. Bain points out that by the time we have reached a degree of concentration as low as this, *"there is a legitimate question as to whether we still have oligopoly."*[5] Finally, with four-firm concentration ratios below 25 percent, "effective joint profit-maximizing action appears unlikely, and competitive market conduct and performance of the sort associated with atomistic market structures might be expected."[6]

One can therefore summarize Bain's conclusions vis-à-vis concentration and the likelihood of tacit cooperation as follows:

Sales of Largest 4 Firms as Share of Market	Likelihood of Tacit Cooperation
76-100%	High
51-75	Moderate
26-50	Low
0-25	Very Low

Bain, if anything, is overly strict in identifying the level of concentration above which tacit collusion can be expected. In advocating a substantial strengthening of the antitrust laws to cope more effectively with market concentration problems, two influential antitrust scholars—Carl Kaysen and Donald Turner, the latter Assistant Attorney General for Antitrust Enforcement (1965-1968)—have made the following recommendations:

> Market power shall be conclusively presumed where, for five years or more, one company has accounted for fifty percent or more of annual sales in the market, or four or fewer companies have accounted for eighty percent of sales. . . .
>
> Adverse effects on competition shall be presumed whenever a company that for five years or more has accounted for twenty percent or more of annual sales in a market acquires any competitor in that market, unless such competitor is insolvent or in obviously declining circumstances.[7]

With the presumption of market power not occurring until a four-firm concentration ratio of 80 percent (or a one-firm market share of 50 percent), Kaysen and Turner are considerably more "liberal" than Bain in their recommendation for a new and stricter antitrust policy.

Other antitrust scholars who have recommended passage of stricter antitrust legislation have also used, as their concentration cut-off point beyond which tacit collusion or market power may be presumed to exist, ratios which are more liberal than the four-firm concentration ratio of 50 percent. In 1967, the White House Task Force on Antitrust Policy was formed to identify the most important areas in which antitrust policy might be strengthened by new legislative or administrative measures. The task force was composed of three lawyers, three economists, and five professors of law, and headed by Phil C. Neal, dean of the University of Chicago Law School. Among the many issues the task force examined was the problem of concentrated markets. The task force felt that current antitrust legislation was inadequate in dealing with these problems, and recommended specific legislation in the form of a Concentrated Industries Act. This act would apply, however, only to "oligopoly industries." An oligopoly industry as defined in the report was one in which:

> (i) any four or fewer firms had an aggregate market share of *seventy percent* or more during at least seven of the ten and four of the most recent five base years; and
>
> (ii) the average market share during the five most recent years of the four firms with the largest average market shares during those base years amounted to at least eighty percent of the average market share of those same four firms during the five preceding base years, . . . [8]

In other words, not only was oligopoly presumed to be absent until a four-firm concentration ratio of *70 percent* had been reached, but stability in the identity of the four leading firms was also required. The inference can therefore be made that, according to this body of experts, industries with four-firm concentration ratios below *50 percent* can in no way be presumed to generate the type of problems normally associated with the existence of market power. (The report went on to further define an oligopoly firm as one whose market share in an oligopoly industry during at least two of the three most recent base years exceeded 15 percent.)

Perhaps one of the strongest attacks on oligopolistic industries has come in the form of the Industrial Reorganization Act (the so-called Hart Bill), which has been before Congress since 1973. However, even this rather restrictive view of how much market concentration should be tolerated holds that a presumption of monopoly power would not be asserted until a four-firm concentration ratio of *50 percent* had been reached. In addition to market concentration, the act would also require the existence of excessive profitability and the absence of price competition.

In conclusion, one can state with considerable confidence that there is a consensus among economists, antitrust law scholars, and public policymakers that a four-firm concentration ratio of 50 percent or less is a cut-off point below which it cannot reasonably be inferred that market power is significant, or that tacit collusion among firms is a likelihood. In the light of this consensus opinion, our structural analysis of the energy industry presented in Chapter Two, using every reasonable industry definition, will clearly show that the level of concentration within this industry does not present problems that should be of concern to public policymakers, and clearly does not present structural problems requiring such a radical departure from our national antitrust policy as industry-specific remedial legislation contemplating large-scale horizontal divestiture of all the major oil companies.

NOTES

1. Eugene M. Singer, *Antitrust Economics: Selected Legal Cases and Economic Models* (Englewood Cliffs, N.J.: Prentice-Hall, 1967), pp. 154-55. (Emphasis added.)

2. Joe S. Bain, *Industrial Organization* (2nd ed.; New York: Wiley, 1968), pp. 135-36.

3. *Ibid.*, p. 136.

4. *Ibid.*

5. *Ibid.*, p. 142.

6. *Ibid.*, pp. 135-36.

7. Carl Kaysen and Donald F. Turner, *Antitrust Policy: An Economic and Legal Analysis* (Cambridge: Harvard University Press, 1959), pp. 98-99.

8. *The Report of the White House Task Force on Antitrust Policy*, [The Neal Paper], p. A-8. As reprinted in the *Journal of Reprints for Antitrust Law and Economics* vol. 1 (Winter 1969):720.

Chapter Two

Concentration in the Energy Industry

In the light of the criteria established in Chapter One, is the level of concentration in the energy industry a legitimate matter of public concern? This is the question to which this chapter is addressed; however, given the many different possible definitions of the energy industry, there is no single concentration ratio that unambiguously measures the current level of concentration therein. Consequently, tables are presented here to show the four-firm, eight-firm, and twenty-firm concentration ratios for all reasonable definitions of the industry.

Before examining these tables it is appropriate to explore the matter of interfuel substitutability and address the question of what is the best definition of an industry. These are two interrelated issues. An appropriate definition of an industry is that it is a group of companies producing "products that are close substitutes to buyers, are available to a common group of buyers, and are relatively distant substitutes for all products not included in the industry."[1] Hence, the question of the degree of interproduct substitutability is immediately raised in the process of ascertaining an industry's level of concentration. This question is exceedingly difficult to answer in the context of the energy industry, and the issue of the prevailing and potential degree of interfuel substitutability is a source of considerable debate. To avoid introducing this source of controversy into our study, therefore, we present here the levels of concentration, given several possible definitions of the industry. Thus, no specific degree of interfuel substitutability is assumed.

It is, however, appropriate to comment on the issue of interfuel substitutability. Those who have testified in opposition to companies diversifying into other sectors of the energy industry maintain that there is a very high degree of interfuel substitutability and that therefore the widest possible industry definition—that is, the energy industry—is the most appropriate. The energy industry thus defined would include petroleum, gas, uranium (for nuclear power), coal, geothermal, and oil shale. In the future, other more esoteric energy sources might also be included. On the other hand, a much narrower definition of the industry is sought by petroleum company managers (and others) who claim that there is either a very low or a zero level of interfuel substitutability. They point out that even in utility markets, where some level of interfuel substitutability is technologically possible, oil and gas are not easily substitutable for coal and uranium, given the latters' costs. Hence oil and gas company executives see literally *an extremely low level of substitutability* between their products and those of coal and uranium producers. Their narrow definition of the industry results in a higher level of concentration than if one used a broader definition—the broader the definition of the industry the lower the prevailing levels of concentration. Given their definition of oil and gas, coal, uranium, and the like as being separate industries, petroleum company executives view their entry into such alternate energy sources as coal, uranium, geothermal, and shale as true *diversifications* into industries whose products are noncompetitive with petroleum company products.

Several energy industry analysts, however—including Federal Trade Commission (FTC) economists—prefer a broad definition of the industry; they maintain that a significant degree of interfuel substitutability exists *at the margin*, and that the rapid pace of technological innovation (liquefaction and gasification of coal, development of automotive engines capable of using fuels other than gasoline, and so on) make the possibility of even greater interfuel substitutability more likely in the future.[2]

With respect to the question, What is the most appropriate geographic basis upon which to construct concentration ratios for the various sectors of the energy industry?, we have chosen to use national ratios for various reasons. The first and most important reason is that the existence of a national energy market seems to be a basic premise of the proposed Interfuel Competition Act introduced in the Senate in 1975. This act would preclude a petroleum company, regardless of how regionalized its petroleum operations were, to own alternate energy resources *anywhere* else. Thus, for example, a petroleum company operating exclusively in, say, the southeastern states would be precluded from owning geothermal deposits in northern California or coal reserves in Montana. The act, therefore, is based upon the assumption that a national energy market exists; hence, national concentration ratios would seem to be appropriate.

Second, apparently the assertion that the energy industry and its various sectors are national rather than regional in scope is consistent with the findings of various economic experts who have addressed themselves to this question. Elzinga and Hogarty developed tests for resolving the thorny problem of geographic market delineation in 1973.[3] Using these tests in an examination of the geographic scope of the energy industry, Hogarty offered the tentative conclusion that "the industries comprising the energy [input] sector—uranium, gas, oil and coal—are [at least] national in scope."[4]

Following in Elzinga and Hogarty's footsteps, Duchesneau examined the various sectors of the energy industry to determine the appropriate geographic boundaries of their markets.[5] Duchesneau found that the natural gas market was indeed national in scope, whereas the crude oil market was "at least national and probably international in scope." For coal, Duchesneau found that his results for 1971 indicated the existence of two U.S. market areas, an eastern and a combined western and central market. His figures for 1971, however, were "more consistent with the presumption of a nationwide market for coal than those for earlier years." A further sign of the expansion in the market scope of coal, he added, was indicated by the increase in exports of coal, especially to the steel industries of Europe and Japan. Technological advances—such as the production of synthetic gas from coal—and improvements in transportation systems and equipment will further expand the scope of the coal industry. Finally, it was completely obvious to Duchesneau that uranium fuels—a highly valued product whose transportation costs represent an insignificant part of their cost—had a market that was at least national in scope.

A further point is that we have confined our analysis of concentration in the energy industry to production and reserves and have not developed ratios for petroleum refining and marketing. Once again this has been done for two reasons. First, for our sequenced structural breakout of the energy industry—from oil to the aggregation of oil, gas, coal, uranium, and geothermal—production and reserves figures alone are appropriate since figures comparable to refining and marketing in the oil industry are meaningless for such sectors as geothermal, coal, and the like. In order to have a common basis for comparison as we move from a narrow to a broad definition of the energy industry, we have therefore restricted our analysis to production and reserve concentration ratios. Second, analysis of the concentration ratios in the refining, transportation, and marketing stages of the petroleum industry brings up the matter of the appropriate level of *vertical integration* that is conducive to competition in an industry. This is indeed a very important question and has been the source of considerable debate and research. It is, however, a distinctly different topic from that of *horizontal diversification* and, therefore, not directly pertinent to a study that focuses on the impact of *horizontal divestiture* on the petroleum industry.[a]

Depending, therefore, upon one's definition of the industry, some of the following tables may be more appropriate than others. The set of tables in toto, however, depicts the level of concentration in the industry under all reasonable definitions—ranging from the narrowest (petroleum alone) to the broadest (the energy industry).

The main conclusion one reaches upon examination of this structural breakout of the energy industry is that, regardless of the industry definition used, the prevailing levels of concentration in the industry are for the most part far below the critical levels generally considered to be of public concern. In other words, given the criteria developed in Chapter One, no matter how one defines the industry, or whether one focuses on production or reserves, the level of concentration is much lower than the cut-off point of a four-firm concentration ratio of 50 percent. Under several definitions of the industry, it appears to be not only unconcentrated, but relatively atomistic. In fact, with the single exception of the uranium sector, the four-firm concentration ratios for the energy industry and its various components are considerably below the 40 to 46 percent average for all 4-digit S.I.C. industries in the U.S. economy.[6]

Table 2-1 presents the four-, eight- and twenty-firm concentration ratios for selected definitions of the energy industry, based on production in BTU equivalents. The range of four-firm concentration ratios is from 18.4 to 26 percent, depending upon the industry definition used. One should note, as we have previously, that this range puts the industry in the classification where Bain asserts that "competitive market conduct and performance of the sort associated with atomistic market structures might be asserted." Table 2-1 also illustrates that, given the broadest industry definition—the one pertinent under the assumption of a reasonably high level of interfuel substitutability—the largest twenty firms produce less than *half* of

---

[a]It can be noted, however, that consideration of the concentration ratios for petroleum refining and marketing developed by other authors does not place the petroleum industry in a different structural classification from the one indicated by our analysis of production and reserve ratios.

Table 2-1. Concentration Ratios Using Selected Definitions of the Energy Industry, Based on Production in BTU Equivalents, 1974[a]

Concentration Ratios[b]	*Energy Industry Definition*				
	Oil[c]	*Oil & Gas*	*Oil & Gas & Coal*	*Oil & Gas & Coal & Uranium*[d]	*Oil & Gas & Coal & Uranium & Geothermal*
4-firm	26.0%	25.1%	19.1%	18.4%	18.4%
8-firm	41.7	39.2	31.5	29.7	29.7
20-firm	61.4	59.0	49.6	47.8	47.8

[a]BTU Heat Equivalent Weights: oil: 5,620,900 BTUs/bbl; natural gas: 1,102,000 BTUs/000 ft^3; coal: 24,580,000 BTUs/short ton; uranium (U_3O_8): 430 billion BTUs/short ton; geothermal: 3,412 BTUs/kilowatt hour (Federal Trade Commission, *Concentration Levels and Trends in the Energy Sector of the U.S. Economy*, 1974, p. 452).

[b]Sources: Calculated from raw data from: FTC, *Concentration Levels and Trends in the Energy Sector of the U.S. Economy, 1974;* corporate annual reports, various issues. "U.S.Coal Production by Company—1974," *Keystone Coal Industry Manual* (New York: McGraw-Hill, 1975); House Committee on Mines and Mining (unpublished data).

[c]Net crude oil, condensate, and natural gas liquids.

[d]Uranium concentrate (yellowcake) production.

the total BTUs. This is indeed a much lower level of concentration than the four-firm 50 percent concentration ratio generally considered to be the critical cut-off point for public policy concern. Finally, one should note that regardless of whether one uses the largest four, eight, or twenty firms, their combined market shares decline as the industry definition expands from oil to the combination of oil, gas, coal, uranium, shale, and geothermal.

Some industry analysts argue that it is the level of concentration in *reserves* and not production that is relevant for any structural analysis of the industry,[7] since reserves are an indicator of potential (future) production. Table 2-2 therefore presents concentration indexes for reserves calculated for the alternative industry definitions used in Table 2-1. Table 2-2 clearly indicates that the ownership of reserves in the energy industry is not highly concentrated; the four-firm concentration ratio range is from 23.4 to 35.1 percent. Even the largest *eight* firms control only 36.6 percent of total reserves—less than the critical 50 percent cut-off point for four-firm concentration discussed earlier. Furthermore, the *identity* (and ranking) of the leading four firms in Table 2-1 is not the same as the largest four reserve holders in Table 2-2. This matter is of considerable importance and will be addressed subsequently at greater length.

Table 2-2. Concentration Ratios for Selected Definitions of the Energy Industry, Based on Privately Controlled Reserves Expressed in BTU Equivalents, 1975[a]

					Energy Industry Definitions	
Concentration Ratios[b]	*Oil*[c]	*Oil & Gas*	*Oil & Gas & Coal*	*Oil & Gas & Coal & Uranium*	*Oil & Gas & Coal & Uranium & Shale Oil*	*Oil & Gas & Coal & Uranium & Shale Oil & Geothermal*
4-firm	35.1%	29.7%	27.4%	26.7%	23.4%	23.4%
8-firm	54.2	45.6	42.8	41.6	36.6	36.6
20-firm	73.1	67.8	67.8	67.2	62.1	62.1

[a]BTU Heat Equivalent Weights: oil: 5,620,900 BTUs/bbl; natural gas: 1,102,000 BTUs/000 ft.3; coal: 24,580,000 BTUs/short ton; uranium (U_3O_8): 430 billion BTUs/short ton; geothermal: 3,412 BTUs/kilowatt hour (Federal Trade Commission, *Concentration Levels and Trends in the Energy Sector of the U.S. Economy*, 1974, p. 452).

[b]Sources: Calculated from raw data from: FTC, *Concentration Levels and Trends in the Energy Sector of the U.S. Economy* 1974; corporate annual reports, various issues. *1975 Coal Mine Directory*, Keystone Coal Industry Manual (New York: McGraw Hill, 1975; Mitchell, Hutchins Inc. (unpublished data); FEA, *Potential Future Role of Oil Shale: Prospects and Constraints*, 1974.

[c]Proven crude oil, condensate, and natural gas liquids; includes Alaskan North Slope.

Finally, we turn to the issue of trends in concentration in the energy industry. Particularly, we project the changes in concentration discernible in the historical data for the purpose of ascertaining whether concentration levels are likely to reach or exceed the critical cut-off point in the foreseeable future. Tables 2-3 through 2-6 present statistics on trends in concentration over the last 20 years in oil, gas, coal, and uranium, respectively. Such trend tables are not presented for shale oil and geothermal, because these fuels are of such recent origin that production has hardly attained commercial scale.

The data in Table 2-3 show that the trend in concentration in crude oil and natural gas liquids production was clearly upward over the period 1955-1970. Since 1970, however, this trend apparently has been halted and, at the four-firm level, possibly reversed; the only increases over the recent time period occurred in the shares of those firms comprising the smallest twelve of the largest twenty petroleum corporations. The percent of production accounted for by the largest four firms actually declined slightly in the 1970-1974 period, while the shares of the largest eight firms remained constant at 41.7 percent.

Table 2-3. U.S. Net Crude Oil, Condensate, and Natural Gas Liquids
Production Concentration Ratios, 1955, 1960, 1965, 1970, 1974

Concentration Ratios	1955	1960	1965	1970	1974
4-firm	18.1%	20.8%	23.9%	26.3%	26.0%
8-firm	30.3	33.5	38.5	41.7	41.7
15-firm	41.0	44.2	50.3	57.1	57.9
20-firm	46.3	49.1	55.0	60.5	61.4

Source: FTC, *Concentration Levels and Trends in the Energy Sector of the U.S. Economy*, 1974; and corporate annual reports.

Table 2-4 presents the same statistics for natural gas production. These data indicate that there has been no clear, consistent trend in concentration in natural gas production. While there has been a modest increase in concentration over the entire period 1955-1974, there have been periods of recession in this trend (1955-1960, 1970-1974). Here again, to the extent that an increase in concentration has occurred, the trend has been more prominent for the smallest twelve of the top twenty firms than for the largest eight; the largest eight firms increased their share of production from 33.1 to 37.2 percent—an increase of 4.1 percent or a relative increase in concentration of *12.4* percent. The remaining twelve firms (of the largest twenty) increased their share of production from 16.4 to 19.4 percent (obtained by subtracting the eight-firm concentration ratios from the twenty-firm concentration ratios for 1955 and 1974, respectively). This represents a 3 percent increase in share of total production accounted for by these firms—a relative increase of *18.3* percent.

Table 2-4. U.S. Net Natural Gas Production Concentration Ratios, 1955, 1960, 1965, 1970, 1974

Concentration Ratios	1955	1960	1965	1970	1974
4-firm	21.7%	16.8%	20.8%	25.2%	24.7%
8-firm	33.1	28.4	33.6	39.1	37.2
15-firm	44.0	39.9	46.0	53.1	51.1
20-firm	49.5	45.0	50.9	58.0	56.6

Source: FTC, *Concentration Levels and Trends in the Energy Sector of the U.S. Economy*, 1974; and corporate annual reports.

Table 2-5.   U.S. Bituminous Coal and Lignite Production Concentration Ratios, 1955, 1960, 1965, 1970, 1974

Concentration Ratio	1955	1960	1965	1970	1974
4-firm	17.8%	21.4%	26.6%	30.7%	26.6%
8-firm	25.5	30.5	36.3	41.2	36.7
15-firm	34.7	39.7	45.6	52.2	46.5
20-firm	39.6	44.5	50.1	56.5	51.2

Source: Derived from data from *Keystone Coal Industry Manual*, "U.S. Coal Production by Company" (New York: McGraw-Hill, various years); U.S. Bureau of Mines, *Mineral Yearbook*, various years.

No matter what the trend has been, however, the largest four firms still produce less than 25 percent of total output, thereby placing the industry in a concentration classification where highly competitive conduct and performance can be expected.

Concentration ratios for coal production for the period 1955-1974 are presented in Table 2-5. While there had been a trend of increasing concentration in the coal industry during the period 1955-1970, this trend was significantly reversed during 1970-1974. However, at no time has the four-firm concentration ratio approached the 50 percent cut-off point, and in 1974 it stood at 26.6 percent. The table also shows that the largest twenty firms accounted for only 51.2 percent of industry output in 1974. Furthermore, of the 5.3 percent reduction in the share of coal production accounted for by the largest twenty companies, which occurred during the period 1970-1974, 4.1 percent (or 77 percent of the total reduction in share) was accounted for by the reduction in the share of the largest four firms.

Finally, Table 2-6 shows concentration ratios for uranium production during the period 1955-1975. The level of concentration in uranium, as might be expected in the case of a relatively new extractive industry, has been higher than in other subsectors of the energy industry. However, since 1955 a significant reduction has occurred in the four-firm and eight-firm concentration ratios. Although the largest four firms still controlled 54.3 percent of uranium production in 1975, this represented a significant reduction from the four-firm concentration ratio of 79.9 percent prevailing in 1955. Furthermore, although eight firms controlled virtually all (99.1 percent) of the industry output in 1955, by 1975, nine firms other than the largest eight had managed to capture a 22.1 percent market share.

Table 2-6. U.S. Uranium Oxide Concentrate Production Concentration
Ratios, 1955, 1960, 1965, 1970, 1975

Concentration Ratios	1955	1960	1965	1970	1975
4-firm	79.9%	51.4%	55.4%	55.3%	54.3%
8-firm	99.1	72.4	79.3	80.8	77.9
15-firm	100.0	94.6	98.1	100.0	N.A.
20-firm	100.0	99.6	100.0	100.0	100.0

Source: FTC, *Concentration Levels and Trends in the Energy Sector of the U.S. Economy*,
1974; House Committee on Mines and Mining.

This significant reduction of concentration in the uranium production has been due, in part, to the entry of petroleum companies into
the industry. Both Exxon and Continental Oil have already begun
uranium production, and other petroleum companies (Getty and
Arco, for example) have announced plans to do likewise. Hence,
petroleum companies' diversification into uranium has been one of
the factors contributing to the reduction in concentration in uranium
production. Further petroleum company diversification, unless pre-
vented by proposed legislation, might be expected to lead to
additional reductions. Indeed, with 85 companies now actively
engaged in exploration while only 17 are currently in mining and
milling, this certainly would be expected to be the case.

In summary, neither the present levels nor the historical trends in
concentration in the oil, gas, coal, and uranium industries are such
that they fall within the range of public policy concern. Where the
trends have been those of increasing concentration, the data show
that concentration levels have fallen far short of a point where
four-firm concentration has approached the 50 percent level. Furthermore, it has frequently been firms other than the largest four
who have enjoyed the largest relative increases in their market shares.
In addition, the concentration ratios for all four industries declined
during the period 1970-1974. In the one industry where concentration is high—uranium production—the trend has been one of significantly decreasing concentration. This trend is attributable in part to
the entry of petroleum companies seeking diversification in the
energy industry, and such trends can be expected to continue as
other petroleum companies enter uranium production. The best way
to insure that trends of increasing concentration do not develop in
any industry is for public policymakers to insure that all industries
are as open to potential entry as possible; arbitrarily excluding

members of one industry from entry into another can only be expected to have an adverse impact upon the structure of that industry. As will be shown in greater detail in Chapter Four, this is especially true in the case of the energy industries under study.

In analyzing trends, considerable emphasis has been given to the fact that for all of the four products considered, the period 1970-1974 gave a picture of *decreasing* four-firm concentration. Before leaving the matter of trends, it might be appropriate to speculate on what the consequences would be if this period were considered an aberration, and that the period 1955-1970 provides the best basis for predicting future trends in concentration. That is, if the trends observed during 1955-1970 reestablish themselves, how long would it take for these industries to approach the four-firm concentration ratio of 50 percent considered to be a relatively strict cut-off point above which the likelihood of tacit collusion becomes a problem? In the oil production industry the four-firm concentration ratio increased by 8.2 percent (from 18.1 to 26.3 percent) during the period 1955-1970. Given the unlikely continuation of an 8.2 percent increase in the four-firm concentration ratio every 15 years, it would still take over 43 years for the four-firm concentration ratio to reach 50 percent. Given the 3.5 percent increase (from 21.7 to 25.2 percent) in the four-firm concentration ratio in the natural gas production industry during the period 1955-1970, it would still take over 107 years for the 50 percent mark to be reached in this industry. Finally, given the 12.9 percent increase in the four-firm concentration ratio for coal production during the 1955-1970 period, it would still take over 27 years for the 50 percent level to be reached. In the case of uranium, of course, the trend uniformly has been one of decreasing concentration by the four largest firms regardless of whether one looks at the 1955-1970 or the 1955-1975 period.

Accordingly, even under the worst case assumption, four-firm concentration ratios of 50 percent cannot be expected in these industries until after the beginning of the twenty-first century. Even if one ignores the reversal of the earlier trend, which occurred in the period 1970-1974, the trend of increasing concentration during the period 1955-1970 would present no structural monopoly problem for public policy for more than a quarter of a century. The energy sector of the U.S. economy is not only relatively unconcentrated but, even under the most pessimistic and unlikely assumptions, is likely to remain so for a long time to come.

Furthermore, it should be noted that mergers were a very important determinant of the increasing trend of concentration in the oil, gas, and coal industries during the 1955-1970 period. Since it is highly unlikely that large mergers will again be permitted to occur between members of these industries, the importance of this source of increasing concentration has been greatly reduced, and an absence of increases in concentration such as those observed during the 1970-1974 period is likely to be the prevailing pattern for the future. In contrast to the cluster of mergers that took place between member firms of various sectors of the energy industry during the 1955-1970 period, a considerable proportion of the recent *diversification* into alternate energy resources by petroleum companies has been effected not by acquisition but through the de novo development of these resources by petroleum firms. Unfortunately, the Interfuel Competition Act of 1975 (S.489) did not seem to take this distinction into consideration. With respect to this point, the director of the Bureau of Competition of the Federal Trade Commission, Owen Johnson, had the following comment to make during his testimony before the Subcommittee on Antitrust and Monopoly of the Senate Judiciary Committee in October 1975:

It is possible that the broadness of S.489 could actually retard growth and development in the alternate energy industries. Potential entrants, having efficient sources of capital, technology and other resources would be precluded from entering these energy fields, even though their entry would not cause any adverse competitive effect. Nor does the bill make any distinction between entry by way of internal expansion or development—which in some cases could be procompetitive—and acquisitions of existing companies and technology.[8]

Further useful insights about the structure of the energy industry can be gained by examination of the *identity* of the leading companies under alternative industry definitions. The twenty top energy producers using selected industry definitions are identified in Table 2-7. It should be noted that the relative rankings of the top energy producers change depending upon the definition of the industry used. Although Exxon, Texaco, and Gulf retain their first, second, and fifth rankings throughout, there is a considerable degree of instability in the ranking of Continental, Kennecott, Shell Oil, and Standard of California, among others. Continental, ranked thirteenth in oil, manages to attain the third highest overall energy ranking due to its coal and uranium operations. Kennecott, absent altogether from the oil and gas industries, is still the seventh largest overall energy producer.

Perhaps even more important than the differences in the identity

Table 2-7.   The Twenty Top Domestic Energy Producers for Selected Energy Industry Definitions, 1974[a]

	Oil	Oil & Gas	Oil & Gas & Coal	Oil & Gas & Coal & Uranium	Oil & Gas & Coal & Uranium Geothermal
Exxon	1	1	1	1	1
Texaco	2	2	2	2	2
Shell Oil	3	4	6	6	6
Standard of Indiana	4	3	3	4	4
Gulf	5	5	5	5	5
Standard of Calif.	6	8	10	10	10
Arco	7	7	9	9	9
Mobil	8	6	8	8	8
Getty Oil	9	11	13	14	14
Union of Calif.	10	9	11	11	11
Sun	11	12	14	15	15
Phillips	12	10	12	13	13
Continental	13	14	4	3	3
Cities Service	14	13	15	17	17
Marathon	15	16	18	20	20
Amerada Hess	16	18	–	–	–
Tenneco	17	15	17	19	19
Louisiana Land	18	●	–	–	–
Superior	19	17	20	–	–
Pennzoil	20	–	–	–	–
Kerr-McGee	–	20	–	12	12
Occidental	–	–	16	18	18
Union Pacific	–	19	–	–	–
Kennecott	–	–	7	7	7
Utah International	–	–	–	16	16

[a]Based on BTU equivalent values.

Source: Calculated from raw data from: FTC, *Concentration Levels and Trends in the Energy Sector of the U.S. Economy*, 1974; corporate annual reports, various issues; "U.S. Coal Production by Company—1974," *Keystone Coal Industry Manual* (McGraw-Hill), 1975; House Committee on Mines and Mining (unpublished data).

and rank of energy producers under alternative industry definitions are the much greater differences existing among energy reserve holders. Since reserves are an indication of long-run production potential, their importance is obvious. Table 2-8 identifies the twenty top energy reserve holders in 1975. Even a cursory examination of the figures in Table 2-8 shows that there is a significant difference in the identities of industry leaders as one expands from a

Table 2-8. The Twenty Top Domestic Energy Reserve Holders for Selected Energy Industry Definitions, 1975[a]

	Oil	Oil & Gas	Oil & Gas & Coal	Oil & Gas & Coal & Uranium	Oil & Gas & Coal & Uranium & Shale Oil	Oil & Gas & Coal & Uranium & Shale Oil & Geothermal
Standard of Ohio	1	3	–	–	16	16
Exxon	2	1	4	4	4	4
Texaco	3	2	15	16	10	10
Arco	4	4	11	13	11	11
Standard of Indiana	5	5	–	–	–	–
Shell	6	6	16	17	18	18
Standard of Calif.	7	7	–	–	17	17
Getty Oil	8	10	–	–	–	–
Gulf	9	8	12	9	7	7
Mobil	10	9	13	14	13	13
Sun	11	13	18	20	–	–
Marathon	12	16	–	–	–	–
Cities Service	13	14	–	–	–	–
Phillips	14	12	20	18	20	20
Union of Calif.	15	11	–	–	–	–
Amerada Hess	16	–	–	–	–	–
Continental	17	18	2	1	1	1
Tenneco	18	17	–	–	–	–
Superior	19	20	–	–	–	–
Louisiana Land	20	–	–	–	–	–
Panhandle Eastern	–	15	–	–	–	–
El Paso	–	19	6	6	6	6
Kerr-McGee	–	–	–	11	14	14
Occidental	–	–	9	10	12	12
Burlington Northern	–	–	1	2	2	2
Union Pacific	–	–	3	3	3	3
Kennecott	–	–	5	5	5	5
Amax	–	–	7	7	8	8
American Natural Gas	–	–	10	12	15	15
U.S. Steel	–	–	14	15	19	19
Eastern Fuel & Gas	–	–	17	19	–	–
N. American Coal	–	–	8	8	9	9
Pacific Power & Light	–	–	19	–	–	–

[a]Based on BTU equivalent values.

Source: Calculated from raw data from: FTC, Concentration Levels and Trends in the Energy Sector of the U.S. Economy, 1974; corporate annual reports, various issues; 1975 Coal Mine Directory, Keystone Coal Industry Manual (New York: McGraw Hill, 1975; Mitchell, Hutchins Inc. (unpublished data); FEA, Potential Future Role of Oil Shale: Prospects and Constraints, 1974.

narrow to a broad definition of the industry. Sohio, the leading reserve holder in the oil industry, is sixteenth in overall energy reserves; while Continental, ranked seventeenth in oil reserves, is the leading overall energy reserve holder. Such large oil reserve holders as Standard of Indiana and Getty Oil do not even appear in the list of the top twenty overall energy reserve holders. Five of the top ten and nine of the top twenty overall energy reserve holders are not even ranked in the list of either the top twenty oil or top twenty oil and gas reserve holders. Finally, of the top ten oil or oil and gas reserve holders, only three are ranked in the list of the top ten overall energy reserve holders.

Previous tables have established that the energy industry is relatively unconcentrated—and to an increasing extent as one expands the definition of the industry. Tables 2-7 and 2-8 further indicate that in addition to being unconcentrated, there is considerable diversity in the identity of the leading firms, especially with respect to reserve holdings, as one expands the definition of the industry. The existence of this considerable degree of asymmetry among leading companies' resources makes the likelihood of tacit collusion even more remote than was inferred earlier from the low level of concentration.[b]

Before concluding our analysis of the level of concentration in the U.S. energy industry it is important to take into consideration the matter of government ownership of energy reserves. To the extent that the government is a holder of energy reserves, our tables of concentration of reserves—which referred only to private sector holdings—have overstated the true level of concentration of energy reserves. Table 2-9 shows that the government is indeed a large holder of energy reserves, holding about half of the coal reserves and over 80 percent of the shale oil and geothermal reserves. By combining the data in Table 2-9 with those on the privately held energy reserves shown in Table 2-2, one can derive figures for the true levels of concentration in total energy reserves, as shown in Table 2-10. These adjusted data indicate that, with the leading four firms accounting for only 10.9 percent of total energy reserves, the industry can scarcely be considered oligopolistic in structure. The 10.9 percent four-firm concentration ratio places the industry's level of concentration somewhat lower than the mid-point of the 0-25 percent concentration range where Bain and other economists predict that the likelihood of tacit collusion is zero and where "competitive market conduct and performance of the sort associated with atomistic market structure might be expected."[9]

---

[b]The implications of this "asymmetry argument" will be more fully explored later on.

Table 2-9. Known Federally and Corporate-Controlled Energy Reserves, 1975

	Nonleased Federal Reserves[a]	*Corporate-Held or -Leased Reserves*	*Total Reserves*	*Ratio, Corporate-Held or -Leased Reserves to Total Reserves*
Oil[b]	11.1×10^9 bbls	39.0×10^9 bbls	50.1×10^9 bbls	77.8%
Natural Gas[b]	negligible	228.2×10^{12} ft^3	228.2×10^{12} ft.^{3}	100
Shale Oil[c]	480×10^9 bbls	120×10^9 bbls	600×10^9 bbls	20.0
Coal[d]	118.4×10^9 tons	131.6×10^9 tons	250×10^9 tons	52.6
Uranium[e]	negliglble	441.5×10^3 tons	441.5×10^3 tons	100
Geothermal[f]	1,146,941 acres	271,408 acres	1,418,349 acres	19.1

[a]Includes nonleased state land and Native American holdings.

[b]Source: American Petroleum Institute (unpublished data). Also assumes Naval Petroleum Reserve No. 9 (Alaska) contains 10 billion barrels. Includes only known reserves, excludes undiscovered but estimated 11-28 billion barrels off-shore thought to exist and be recoverable in addition to undiscovered gas deposits, all on federally controlled lands.

[c]Source: FEA, *Project Independence Task Force Report on Oil Shale*, November 1974.

[d]Conservatively based on Exxon estimate of 250×10^9 tons recoverable proven coal reserves. Government estimates are much higher: Bureau of Mines, May 1975, 437×10^9 tons recoverable; FEA Project Independence, 390×10^9 tons economically recoverable.

[e]Based on Mitchell Hutchins, Inc. and petroleum-company-supplied data, together with FEA's 1976 *National Energy Outlook* (FEA-N-75/713).

[f]Of 1,418,349 acres classified by the U.S. geological survey as "Known Thermal Resource Acres" in the state of California, 271,408 are accounted for by oil company lease holdings. Testimony before the California Senate Committee on Public Utilities, Transit and Energy, May 4, 1976, by Carel Otte, V.P., Union Oil Company.

Some have urged that it is essential, in analyzing the structure of the petroleum industry, to take into consideration the impact of joint ventures on the degree of competition prevailing in the industry. We have not done so for two reasons. First, it is not entirely clear whether joint ventures are procompetitive or anticompetitive in nature. What is clear, however, is that, if found to be anticompetitive, joint ventures can be dealt with through existing antitrust statutes. With reference to this point, Assistant Attorney General Thomas Kauper of the Antitrust Division of the Department of Justice had the following to say during his testimony before Congress:

It is, of course, always possible that a joint venture will produce anticompetitive consequences, either actual or potential. I believe that existing antitrust enforcement authority is quite sufficient to allow careful analysis of such situations and, where appropriate, to enjoin their creation or continuation.[10]

Table 2-10.   Concentration Ratios for Selected Definitions of the Energy Industry,
Based on Privately and Publicly Controlled Reserves Expressed in BTU Equivalents,
1975[a] (expressed as percent)

Concentration Ratios[b]	Oil[c]	Oil & Gas	Oil & Gas & Coal	Oil & Gas & Coal & Uranium	Oil & Gas & Coal & Uranium & Shale Oil	Oil & Gas & Coal & Uranium & Shale Oil & Geothermal
4-firm	27.3	26.2	15.2	15.1	10.9	10.9
8-firm	42.2	40.3	23.7	23.6	17.8	17.4
20-firm	56.9	59.9	37.6	38.1	29.0	29.0

[a]BTU Heat Equivalent Weights: oil: 5,620,900 BTUs/bbl; natural gas: 1,102,000 BTUs/000 ft^3; coal: 24,580,000 BTUs/short ton; uranium (U_3O_8): 430 billion BTUs/short ton; geothermal: 3,412 BTUs/kilowatt hour (Federal Trade Commission, *Concentration Levels and Trends in the Energy Sector of the U.S. Economy*, 1974, p. 452).

[b]Calculated from raw data from: FTC, *Concentration Levels and Trends in the Energy Sector of the U.S. Economy, 1974*; corporate annual reports, various issues; *1975 Coal Mine Directory*, Keystone Coal Industry Manual (New York: McGraw Hill, 1975; Mitchell, Hutchins Inc. (unpublished data); American Petroleum Institute (unpublished data); FEA *Potential Future Role of Oil Shale: Prospects and Constraints*, 1974; FEA *1976 National Energy Outlook* (FEA-N-75/713); Testimony before the California State Committee on Public Utilities, Transit and Energy, May 4, 1976 by Carel Otte, V.P., Union Oil Company; and the Submission of Exxon company, U.S.A. before the House Judiciary Subcommittee on Monopolies and Commercial Law, September 11, 1975.

[c]Proven crude oil, condensate, and natural gas liquids; includes Alaskan North Slope.

Second, and of considerable importance, is the fact that the existence of joint ventures will not be affected by the passage of horizontal divestiture legislation. Joint ventures could still exist even after passage of such legislation. Hence, it seems inappropriate to dwell upon the topic of joint ventures in a study aimed at discussing the potential impact of horizontal divestiture upon the petroleum industry.

The analysis of the structural data presented in this chapter support the following conclusions about concentration levels and trends in the energy sector of the U.S. economy:

- *No matter what industry definition is used, the levels of concentration in the U.S. energy industry are relatively moderate and are nowhere near the cut-off point above which problems of tacit collusion or monopoly are likely to occur.*

- *The broader the definition used—and those who find a high degree of interfuel substitutability argue for a very broad industry definition—the lower the level of concentration in the industry.*

- *Even if one ignores the period 1970-1974, a period during which concentration levels in the industry were reduced, the trends in concentration-level increases that occurred during the period 1955-1974 do not present any problems of immediate concern to public policy. The number of years required before these levels would carry the industry past the most restrictive possible danger point range, for various sectors of the industry, from 27 to 107 years. Furthermore, the likely absence of significant merger activity in the industry make it unlikely that such trends will continue.*

- *When the identities of the leading firms are examined sector by sector, especially with respect to reserves, a considerable degree of asymmetry is revealed. The difference between current industry leaders in production and those firms that can reasonably be expected to be the industry leaders of the future because of their reserve holdings is significant. Hence one can expect a considerable degree of "competitive turbulence" in the industry over time.*

- *When allowance is made for the energy reserve holdings of the government, the level of concentration in several sectors of the industry declines dramatically. With such reserves in its possession the government possesses a very potent force for affecting the structure of the industry.*

Our conclusions, it should be pointed out, do not conflict with statements coming from sources that can be expected to be highly sensitive to the energy industry's structure. In the conclusion to the FTC's 1974 report *Concentration Levels and Trends in the Energy Sector of the U.S. Economy*, the following statement appears:

> The information reported in this study appears to suggest that petroleum company acquisitions into coal companies up to 1970 may not have had a severe impact on energy production concentration. Consequently, *this study does not provide any positive support for the proposal that petroleum companies be banned from acquiring coal or uranium companies; nor does it suggest that petroleum companies be banned from acquiring coal or uranium reserves.*[11]

Appearing before the Joint Economic Committee in November 1975, F.M. Scherer, then chief economist at the Federal Trade Commission, in discussing horizontal divestiture, stated that in his opinion the levels of concentration in the combined energy market "do not yet approach the peril point."[12] Assistant Attorney General Thomas E. Kauper of the Antitrust Division, in a statement presented to the Senate Judiciary Committee on June 8, 1976 about the proposed Petroleum Industry Competition Act of 1976 (the so-called Vertical Disintegration Act) stated:

> ... The petroleum industry appears to be one of the least concentrated of our nation's major industries. *This data calls into question the propriety of massive structural reorganization. If the present structure of the industry does not exhibit the characteristics associated with excessive market power, then a solution based upon that premise may be both unavailable and counterproductive.*[13]

Finally, Owen Johnson, director of the FTC's Bureau of Competition, in testimony before the Senate Subcommittee on Antitrust and Monopoly on October 21, 1975, commented upon the Interfuel Competition Act of 1975 (S.489) as follows:

> The basic conclusion of that study [the 1974 FTC study, *Concentration Levels and Trends in the Energy Sector of the U.S. Economy*] is that we have no positive data that would justify a ban on petroleum companies acquiring coal or uranium companies or coal and uranium reserves; ... S.489 is described as a "competition act" and an amendment to the antitrust laws. However, the business relationships which it proscribes would, in effect, be irrebuttably presumed to be anticompetitive. This inflexible approach is certainly not a traditional antitrust resolution of competitive problems.[14]

NOTES

1. Joe S. Bain, *Industrial Organization* (2nd ed.; New York: Wiley, 1968), p. 124.

2. FTC, *Concentration Levels and Trends in the Energy Sector of the U.S. Economy*, 1974, p. 19.

3. K. Elzinga and T. Hogarty, "The Problem of Geographic Market Delineation in Antimerger Suits," *Antitrust Bulletin* 18 (Spring 1973):45-82.

4. T. Hogarty, "The Geographic Scope of the Energy Markets: Oil, Gas and Coal," in Thomas D. Duchesneau, *Competition in the U.S. Energy Industry* (Cambridge: Ballinger Publishing Company, 1975), Appendix A.

5. T.D. Duchesneau, *Competition in U.S. Energy Industry*, pp. 29-35.

6. F.M. Scherer, *Industrial Market Structure and Economic Performance* (Chicago: Rand McNally, 1970), p. 63.

7. Cf. testimony of John W. Wilson before U.S. Senate Committee on the Judiciary Subcommittee on Antitrust and Monopoly, Washington, D.C., June 27, 1973, p. 15 (mimeographed copy).

8. "Hearings before the Subcommittee on Antitrust and Monopoly of the Committee on the Judiciary, United States Senate, October 21, 1975," p. 308.

9. J.S. Bain, *Industrial Organization*, pp. 135-36.

10. "Hearings before the Subcommittee on Antitrust and Monopoly of the Committee on the Judiciary, United States Senate, October 22, 1975," p. 348.

11. Federal Trade Commission, *Concentration Levels and Trends in the Energy Sector of the U.S. Economy*, 1974, pp. 260-61. (Emphasis added.)

12. Joint Economic Committee: Horizontal Integration of the Energy Industry. November 19, 1975, p. 75.

13. Thomas M. Kauper. Senate Judiciary Committee. The Petroleum Industry: S. 2387, June 8, 1976, p. 60. (Emphasis added.)

14. "Hearings before the Subcommittee on Antitrust and Monopoly of the Committee on the Judiciary, United States Senate, October 21, 1975," p. 308.

 *Chapter Three*

Assessment of Oil Company Behavior in Relation to Development of Alternative Energy Resources

The earlier sections of this study addressing the present structure of the energy industry lead to the conclusion that at present, and for the foreseeable future, the energy industry is not sufficiently concentrated to warrant special congressional action. Yet the issue at hand may be much broader than that of antitrust and market concentration. For example, in his opening statement before the Subcommittee of Energy of the U.S. Congress Joint Economic Committee on December 8, 1975, Senator Edward Kennedy stated:

> I am struck by the inadequacy of any analysis of oil industry structure that is limited to traditional and anti-trust considerations or narrow definitions of what supposedly constitutes a competitive market structure. The issue that now confronts Congress by the acquisition of competing energy sources by major oil companies cannot be resolved simply by counting the number of companies and their energy subsidiaries and comparing this number to what exists in other, quite different, industries. One must look very carefully at the end result of the process where alternative energy sources are increasingly controlled by what could be described as energy conglomerates.

This chapter is designed to do precisely what Senator Kennedy proposes by projecting from present patterns of behavior the most likely end results of the petroleum companies' investment in alternative energy sources. The resulting analysis supports the following general conclusions.

Pricing.—Given the structure of the energy industries, no single petroleum company owning either coal or uranium subsidiaries is able to control prices of the various alternative energy sources. These, absent overt agreements, are set by market forces. Increases in the number of competitors resulting from the entry of petroleum companies into each of these energy markets make them more rather than less competitive.

Capital Investment.—In view of potential capital shortages and the huge amounts of risk capital necessary to develop potential future energy sources, the petroleum companies are not only prime sources but may well be the only potential major private source of these capital outlays.

R&D.—Research efforts are somewhat enhanced by large firm size; and significant areas of synergy exist between research in various energy resource areas.

Technology Transfer.—There is an actively functioning licensing system within the petroleum industry which encourages effective, efficient R&D, and which moves technology quickly from the patent stage to commercialization of the more attractive patents. This practice not only helps the larger companies support their core R&D functions but also allows for many smaller companies to have access to modern technology with only minimal or no R&D core functions themselves.

Asymmetry among Firms.—Significant asymmetry exists among petroleum firms. Continued diversification of petroleum firms in alternative energy resource areas would enhance such asymmetry. Because asymmetry is procompetitive, efforts to restrict such expansion may be expected to have anticompetitive implications.

Artificial Production Constraints.—In an economy where demand is increasing more rapidly than available domestic supply, given the structure of the industry, it is not to any profit-maximizing energy firm's advantage to artificially restrict production. Under these conditions a withholding of production is inconsistent with rational economic behavior.

THE RESEARCH DATA BASE

The analysis leading to the foregoing general conclusions involved a synthesis of data obtained from the following sources.

Questionnaires

A confidential questionnaire distributed to twenty-three petroleum companies, all of whom responded, provided the following data:

- Total R&D expenditures by year for the last five years and projections for the next five years broken down by energy source, dollar expenditure, and, where available, personnel allocation.
- Licensing policies and revenues from existing licenses.
- Technology presently in use in alternative energy sources that have been originated and developed for their petroleum operations.
- New processes or techniques not now in use but in preparatory stages for use in development of alternative energy sources.

Since these individual company data are confidential, they had to be used in aggregate form. Only in cases where projects and costs are in the public record, or where companies have agreed to disclosure, are company data identified. The requirement that individual company data not be disclosed does not materially reduce the value of the information for the purposes of our analysis.

While there are certain shortcomings in the data which should be noted, they do not seriously impair the data's usefulness: (1) R&D as reported by the majority of the twenty-three responding companies includes research and laboratory development but does not include funds invested in development of potentially commercially viable projects. This tends to understate their total R&D expenditures. (2) A few companies reported total data for the period 1971-1974, and yearly data only for 1975. Thus, annual data for the years 1971 through 1974 will not reflect expenditures for all companies. (3) In some cases it is unclear whether the reported revenues from licensing are exclusively for energy-related technology or include those resulting from the licensing of petrochemical processes. A comparison of the questionnaire data with licensing revenues reported in annual reports revealed that all companies do not report on a consistent basis. Despite these shortcomings the data are probably the most complete breakout of oil company R&D expenditures and policies compiled to date.

Interviews

In the course of this study we interviewed over thirty top executives in the energy industry. This field research covered a cross-section of top corporate executives of petroleum companies, general managers of both oil company R&D departments and of coal and uranium divisions of petroleum companies, and top executives of independent coal companies. The companies were chosen by a random selection process designed to include a cross-section of large and small companies with significant coal or uranium holdings. These interviews provided necessary background material and furnished insights into different corporate perspectives and strategies regarding method and rationale for planning decisions in the areas of R&D and pricing while probing for the desired outcomes of various investment strategies. The interviews with presidents of independent coal companies provided a major input to the section on differential product pricing and competition among selected energy sources, and served the useful purpose of gaining the perspectives and opinions of managers of nonpetroleum companies. The interviews with heads of R&D divisions focused on the areas of technology transfer and synergy, and served as a vehicle for understanding the extremely complicated technical material that surfaced in literature searches on patents, licenses, and existing alternative energy technologies.

Published Data Search

All available scientific and economic data published by government and reliable private sources were screened for material relevant to the issues the study sought to cover. In addition, a thorough patent search was conducted in the areas of coal conversion and oil shale technology. This was supplemented by an overall patent search done by computer by the American Petroleum Institute's abstracting service.

ALTERNATIVE ENERGY SOURCE PRICE COMPETITION

It is axiomatic in economic theory that up to a point the more competitors present in a given marketplace, the stronger price competition tends to become. Because price competition is held to be generally beneficial to society, the motivation behind much of the legislation comprising public policy toward industry is to increase the vigor of competition by increasing the number of competitors in any given market.

In order to measure the number of competitors in a market, however, it is first necessary to define the bounds of that market. In regard to the energy industry it would appear that currently in only one market are the various forms of energy sufficiently substitutable to be of interest to us here.[1] That market is, of course, the utility fuel market.

In general, technological factors limit the degree of interfuel substitutability to a greater extent in other energy consumption sectors. Constraints on substitutability are most pronounced in the transportation sector where petroleum products maintain a virtual monopoly due to the characteristics of the fuel burning equipment used there.[2]

A significant degree of interfuel competition does exist, however, in the residential, commercial and industrial sectors. A chief element in the latter areas is the role of electricity as an energy input. Use of electricity greatly extends the range of interfuel competition since all four fuels compete to supply electric utilities even if they do not compete directly in the consumption sectors supplied by electricity.[3]

Because of the lack of fuel substitutability in other fields of energy utilization (transportation, commercial, industrial, residential), the entrance of additional competitors, whatever their other industry interests, into these markets should be considered procompetitive. Indeed, these areas are almost entirely oil- and gas-based anyway, according to the FTC Staff Report.[4] A condensed version of their analysis of fuel utilization by consumption sector is presented in Table 3-1. It is apparent that only the industrial and electric utility sectors are users of nonpetroleum-based fuels. In the industrial sector approximately 56 percent of all coal used in 1974[5] was of the nonsubstitutable metallurgical type necessary for steelmaking, significantly diminishing the importance of this consumption sector to our study. Furthermore, the amount of coal in this sector considered substitutable has been rapidly decreasing over time and is expected to continue doing so.[6] Table 3-2 illustrates the decrease in the industrial sector's (excluding metallurgical) consumption since 1935. Only in the utility area, which accounted for 27 percent of total domestic energy utilization in 1974,[7] is the substitutability of

Table 3-1. Percent Utilization of Primary Fuels by Consumption Sector, 1970

	Electric Utilities[a]	*Residential/ Commercial*	*Industrial*	*Transportation*
Oil & Gas	44.4%	97.7%	75.6%	100.0%
Coal	54.0	2.3	24.4	0.0
Uranium	1.7	0.0	0.0	0.0
	100.0%	100.0%	100.0%	100.0%

[a]Total does not add to 100.00 due to rounding.

Source: FTC, *Concentration Levels and Trends in the Energy Section of the U.S. Economy*, 1974, p. 6.

Table 3-2. Annual Industrial and Total Consumption of Bituminous Coal, 1935-1975 (in thousands of tons)[a]

Year	Industrial Consumption	Total Consumption	Industrial as Percent of Total Consumption
1935	175,163	366,058	47.8
1940	198,553	447,376	44.3
1945	255,885	587,523	43.5
1950	164,754	479,670	34.3
1955	113,613	474,689	23.9
1960	86,804	416,970	20.8
1961	84,895	409,375	20.7
1962	86,485	426,187	20.2
1963	90,935	456,303	19.9
1964	91,607	479,085	19.1
1965	94,487	509,345	18.5
1966	98,481	535,568	18.3
1967	93,464	539,944	17.3
1968	92,028	549,457	16.7
1969	85,374	563,509	15.1
1970	82,909	586,563	14.1
1971	68,655	551,495	12.4
1972	67,131	572,736	11.7
1973	60,837	608,892	9.4
1974	57,819	612,635	9.4
1975	48,694	512,454	9.5

[a]Excludes metallurgical coal; 1975 data through October.

Source: President's Council on Wage and Price Stability, *A Study of Coal Prices*, 1976.

energy sources sufficient to raise the question of the desirability of multi-resource energy companies. The effect of multisource energy companies on utility fuel price competition depends on three criteria: (1) various utility fuels must be substitutable; (2) the economic incentive for "non-arms-length" fuel pricing must be present; and (3) it must be physically possible for producing companies to substitute one fuel for another. If none of these criteria are met, it follows that multi-energy resource companies provide a procompetitive pricing force not only in nonutility markets, but in utility energy markets as well, through the addition of new sellers in the marketplace.

Utility Fuel Substitutability

The perfect substitutability of utility fuels in a competitive market would dictate identical prices among fuels after adjustment for differences among them in operating and capital charges. This means that price parallelism, given perfect substitutability, would be absolute. Thus, for example, any fluctuation in the price of utility fuel oil would be matched by a comparable fluctuation in the price of steam coal and vice versa. At the other extreme, a lack of product substitutability should be indicated by a relatively low correlation among price movements.[8]

Of all the different energy sources listed for divestiture under S.489, oil and coal have been held to be the most substitutable by the Federal Trade Commission:

> More so than any other fuel consumer, an electric utility possesses a great deal of flexibility in its choice of fuels. The bulk of electricity is produced by steam generating plants that are capable of using any fossil fuel (coal, gas, or fuel oil) either singly or in combination. In a long run context, uranium enters as a viable alternative since utilities have a choice of building either a conventional steam plant or a nuclear facility where electricity is generated by a reactor that uses nuclear fuel.[9]

Similarly, David Schwartzman, in his analysis of the cross-elasticity of demand between fuels, found that only residual oil is a substitute for coal:

> The competitive relationship between coal and each of the following has been analyzed: residual oil, natural gas, and uranium oxide. The analysis concludes that only residual oil is a substitute for coal.[10]

For this reason, the following analysis is concerned with oil and coal prices.

Because the period since 1973 has been one of dynamic change in the pricing of utility fuels, and because the petroleum industry's involvement in coal is a relatively recent phenomena, the time frame 1973 through 1975 was chosen for detailed analysis. Table 3-3 presents average fuel-oil and steam-coal cost data as compiled by the Federal Power Commission.[11] Because utilities purchase both coal and oil predominantly on a long-term contractual basis (about 80 percent of their volume), the numbers shown are weighted toward such contract averages; however, they also include, in both cases, the cost of short-term supplies purchased on a spot basis. The data indicate that although coal prices to utilities increased dramatically

Table 3-3.   Average Monthly Delivered Cost—Electric Utility Fuel Oil and
Coal, April 1973-October 1975

| Month | Year | Fuel Oil | | Steam Coal | | Ratio of Oil |
		$/bbl	Index	$/ton	Index	to Coal Indexes
April	1973	$4.22	100	$8.80	100	1.00
May	1973	4.31	102	8.80	100	1.02
June	1973	4.28	101	8.94	102	0.99
July	1973	4.42	105	8.82	100	1.05
August	1973	4.69	111	8.84	100	1.11
September	1973	4.89	116	9.10	103	1.13
October	1973	5.32	126	9.35	106	1.19
November	1973	6.24	149	9.74	111	1.34
December	1973	7.34	174	10.00	114	1.52
January	1974	9.77	231	11.32	129	1.79
February	1974	11.42	271	12.53	142	1.91
March	1974	11.58	275	11.37	152	1.81
April	1974	11.49	272	13.84	157	1.73
May	1974	11.58	274	14.46	164	1.67
June	1974	11.96	283	15.17	172	1.65
July	1974	11.92	282	15.88	180	1.57
August	1974	11.93	283	16.74	190	1.49
September	1974	11.94	283	17.19	195	1.45
October	1974	12.17	288	17.58	200	1.44
November	1974	12.26	291	19.23	219	1.32
December	1974	12.54	297	18.78	213	1.39
January	1975	12.19	289	17.41	198	1.46
February	1975	12.44	295	17.71	201	1.47
March	1975	12.58	298	17.50	199	1.50
April	1975	12.79	303	17.52	199	1.52
May	1975	12.61	249	17.78	202	1.48
June	1975	12.31	292	17.65	200	1.46
July	1975	12.25	290	17.23	196	1.48
August	1975	12.38	293	17.71	201	1.46
September	1975	12.39	294	17.81	202	1.46
October	1975	12.19	289	17.73	201	1.44

Source: Council on Wage and Price Stability, *A Study of Coal Prices*, 1976.

between April 1973 (pre-oil embargo levels) and October 1975, they
did not begin to keep pace with the increase in oil prices. The ratio
of the average utility fuel oil cost to that of average utility steam coal
cost increased almost 50 percent over the entire period, and at one
point had increased to over 90 percent (in February 1974, fuel oil

costs were, relative to coal costs, almost twice as high as they had been in April of 1973), before being forced down due to an increase in coal prices caused by inventory buying prior to the United Mine Workers strike of 1974.[1 2] Coal prices, therefore—although certainly increasing in the same direction as oil prices—were hardly increasing strictly in parallel. This observation leads one to the conclusion that, at best, fuel oil and steam coal are imperfect substitutes for one another.

This imperfection is attributable to several factors. Utilities cannot and do not switch at will from one fuel source to another, because of technological constraints (plant considerations), environmental constraints (pollution-control requirements),[1 3] legal constraints (fulfillment of long-term contracts), and managerial constraints (the logistics and skills involved in handling fuel oil are a great deal different from those involved in handling coal). Indeed, more than half the fossil-fuel-burning plants are limited to burning either oil, gas, or coal for technological reasons alone.[1 4] Furthermore, there are significant costs associated with fuel conversion even when this is technologically feasible. Between 1965 and 1972, 398 coal-fired boilers, representing about 7 percent of the total generating capacity of the United States, were converted to the use of oil. Even to reconvert the 80 percent of such boilers back to coal where reconversion is possible was estimated to cost (in 1973) in excess of $100 million.[1 5]

While in the past utility fuel substitutability was hindered for the above reasons, the future will add still another—government restriction. Section 2 of the Energy Supply and Environmental Coordination Act of 1974 (ESECA) requires the Federal Energy Administration (FEA) to prohibit any power plant from burning oil or gas when it can practically burn coal and meet the Environmental Protection Agency (EPA) air-pollution requirements. Furthermore, the FEA may require power plants in the early planning stage to be designed to use coal as the primary energy source. On this basis the FEA had issued orders requiring the conversion of 74 units to coal (at an estimated cost of $300 million) as of April 29, 1974, and construction orders requiring an additional 74 units to utilize coal as the primary energy source.

For new plant construction, utilities will be unable to obtain natural gas. Further, utilities will be allowed to burn oil only when the use of oil is consistent with ESECA, that is, only if it is impractical to burn coal. In sum, no new utilities will burn natural gas and some new utilities will burn oil, but only because it is not practicable to burn coal.

Thus, due to recently enacted regulations and changed market circumstances vis-à-vis natural gas, interfuel substitutability in electrical generation is becoming significantly limited, particularly substitutability between coal and oil or natural gas. Therefore, the answer to the question of meeting the first criterion (product substitutability) must be termed as limited at best.

Economic Feasibility

For petroleum companies to set their coal (or other energy resource) prices at other than the market-dictated levels requires that they individually have both the market power and an economic incentive to do so. The most often-advanced argument showing that the requisite incentive exists goes something like this: No logical business would deliberately undercut the price of its major product in the marketplace. To do so would be financially harmful and could be disastrous. However, this is exactly what would be expected of the petroleum companies if they were required to compete freely in the steam-coal marketplace with independent coal companies. However, oil companies with coal operations will not price their coal at BTU equivalent dollar values cheaper than that of their oil. Such companies will therefore not be a procompetitive pricing force in the coal marketplace, and may have the effect of lessening price competition in the energy industry generally.

Superficially, at least, this may make a rather attractive argument. However, it breaks down when analyzed more closely. Because most coal moves under long-term contracts, any reduction in coal prices would only affect sales under negotiation, not those already consummated (assuming the reduction was not a cost reduction pass-through). Thus incremental analysis is applicable. Conoco, the parent of the largest coal subsidiary (Consolidation) of any oil firm, has only a 2 percent share of the total U.S. oil market. Conoco, if it sacrifices any of its coal sales by refusing to lower prices, could, on a U.S. average basis, expect to recover only an insignificant percent of such foregone coal sales revenues in the form of increased oil sales. Thus, for Conoco simply to break even, its increased profits on the incremental oil sales generated must be about fifty times its profits on the coal sales foregone (in terms of dollars profit per BTU). Actually, as will be shown later on, Conoco could expect to recover even less than the 2 percent expected share of the resultant petroleum sales due to the fact that its steam coal and fuel marketing areas do not, by and large, overlap. Even for Exxon, the largest oil company in the United States, such a pricing policy probably would never be considered in its financial interests. Exxon, with its 8.5 percent share of the U.S. petroleum market, would have to be gathering profits per BTU equivalent of oil on the order of twelve times that which it gets for its coal.

The argument has been advanced, however, that because of the assumed cooperative—rather than competitive—nature of oil firms, one cannot look at individual company economics but must look at the impact of competitive pricing as it relates to the group as a whole. Thus, even if Conoco loses revenue because Consolidation maintains its coal prices, some other oil company will gain this revenue from the sale of oil. In aggregate, then, the industry will stand to gain by refraining from offering coal (or oil) at lower prices than those at which it sells its oil (or coal). Even if one assumes, for argument's sake, that all petroleum companies act as a tight-knit oligopoly,[16] application of some elementary financial analysis shows the preceding theory to be invalid. The top twenty oil producers account for only slightly over 10 percent of total U.S. coal production, and control less than 30 percent of all privately held coal reserves (less than 15 percent of all coal reserves). Thus, any concerted action of price stabilization by this group of coal producers could only result in non-oil coal producers acquiring additional business. The relatively small market power of the oil company coal subsidiaries (even in aggregate) and the difficulty and expense of short-term substitution would make concerted action on the part of oil companies to maintain coal prices *not* result in utilities switching from coal to oil, but from *their* coal to other coal. This was summed up pragmatically by the chief executive officer of one of the three largest independent coal producers in the United States when in reference to a specific western area, he stated to us:

> Continental is selling coal for less than four dollars [a ton]. We just love to take their business. We've four billion tons of reserves up there,—they have one.[17]

Although the prevailing market structure and nonsubstitutability of oil and coal alone are enough to insure that petroleum companies act competitively in coal pricing, the additional factor of transportation costs lends even more weight to this conclusion. Coal production is projected to increase from its 1975 level of 604 million tons in 1974 to approximately a billion tons annually by 1985.[18] Most of this increase (anywhere up to 75 percent) is projected to come from fields located west of the Mississippi.[19] Even by 1980, it is anticipated that 30 to 40 million tons of Wyoming coal will be consumed annually by utility plants in southern and midwestern states located 800 to 1,500 miles from the coal fields of eastern Wyoming.

There are four basic alternatives open for coal transportation from these fields to energy-consuming regions. Due to technological, economic, or other reasons, three of these four are either partially or completely closed to coal companies.

1. Mine-Mouth Power Plants and EHV Transmission Lines. This alternative requires the presence of an adequate supply of cooling water near the mine site. Western coal mines do not have this resource available in most cases. Further, if the new amendment of the Clean Air Act on nondegradation policy is approved, power plants will have to be equipped with very efficient scrubbers, making the investment less attractive.

But further, the economics show that EHV transmission is only attractive within a 500-mile radius from the power source. It appears, therefore, that this alternative would not be attractive for long-distance hauls of energy, although it may be used for power transmission within the western region.

2. Barge Movement. For water movements of coal, jumbo barges of 1,500 tons are used in tows of 30,000 tons. Barge rates for coal are around 0.3¢/ton-mile, making barging the most economical way of hauling coal. But the nearest navigable portion of the Missouri River is 400 to 600 miles away from the coal fields. The Missouri, with channel depths of 9 feet or less, is not ideal for coal traffic, limiting jumbo barges to maximum loads of 900 tons; in channel depths of 9 feet or more, barges can handle 1,400 to 1,500 tons. Furthermore, ice usually closes the Missouri between December and February.

The lower Mississippi-Ohio-Tennessee river system presents ideal conditions for bulk transport movements, but there are some questions about lock capacity. The upper Mississippi and Illinois waterway systems present icing problems that would limit traffic. The Great Lakes also have traffic limitations between December and March.

3. Slurry Pipelines. A number of the anticipated western coal-mine-to-generating-plant complexes appear to be large enough to make the coal slurry pipeline a viable alternative. Coal slurry pipelines present the advantage of hauling coal at a low cost, mostly for high-volume/long-distance hauls. Further, they offer a guarantee against transportation cost escalation, as about 70 percent of pipeline tariffs are capital-related charges. Although costs depend on terrain, it is expected that a Wyoming-to-Arkansas pipeline could operate at 0.5-0.6¢/ton-mile, at a volume of 25 million tons per year.

However, pipelines present a significant environmental problem because they would need huge amounts of water (the planned Arkansas pipeline would carry 17 million U.S. gallons of water per day). Also, a battle rages between slurry pipeline proponents and railroads over the issue of providing pipelines the right of eminent domain. As long as railroads hold such rights, pipelines—which would have to cross many railroad tracks—cannot be developed. The railroads are trying to demonstrate that pipelines would take the cream of the western coal transportation market, leaving them with only the smaller movements requiring rail flexibility.

4. **Rail Movement.** Currently, the only feasible method for moving the bulk of the coal from western reserves is rail, the means most in use today. In 1974 some 600 million tons of coal were produced in the United States, and the railways moved 388 million tons, about 65 percent of the total. Of this tonnage, 135 million tons (about 29 percent) moved in unit trains.

Unit trains are dedicated freight trains made up of between 100 and 170 cars that are for the exclusive delivery of coal to a specific customer's plant at a special low freight rate. The number of cars varies with delivery rate and the terrain over which the train must travel. Even so, they represent an extremely high cost of transportation in proportion to the cost of coal at the mine mouth. In 1974, unit train rates for coal movements of 1,100 miles (from Billings, Montana to Kansas City) was $11.70 per ton, compared to a mining cost of between $2-3 per ton. For western coal being delivered to Detroit Edison, rail costs are estimated at $13-15 per ton, versus a $7 per ton price on the coal. These transportation costs are a quantum jump over what was incurred for eastern coal (see Table 3-4), and even eastern coal was recognized to have a higher associated transportation cost than any other energy form:

> Transportation costs are more significant for coal than for any of the other major fuels. For example, in 1970 the average value per ton of bituminous coal or lignite at the mine was $6.26, and the average railroad freight charge for class I railroads was $3.41 per ton. In other words, the average rail transportation rate was 54.5 percent of the price of coal at the mine or about 35.3 percent of the delivered price of coal.[20]

For western coal, of course, the delivered costs are significantly higher. Assuming the data given in Table 3-4 are representative, transportation cost would be 75 percent of the cost of delivered western coal, or 300 percent of the cost of coal at the mine mouth. In comparison to the cost of oil with the highest transportation

Table 3-4.   Delivered Cost of Eastern and Western Coals, Western Pennsylvania Utility, 1975

	Eastern	Western
Quality		
BTU/lb	13,000	8,500
Percent Sulfur	2.5	0.5
KWH/Ton	2,900	1,700
Mine-Price ($/Ton)	25.00	5.00
Transportation ($/Ton)	3.00	15.00
Delivered Cost		
$/Ton	28.00	20.00
$/Million BTUs	1.08	1.18
Mills/KWH (W/O Scrubbing)	9.7	13.6
Mills/KWH (W/Scrubbing)	13.8	13.6

Source: T.G. Norris, V.P. Planning and Economics, Consolidation Coal Company, "The Coal Outlook: Industry Perspective," presentation to Security Analysts, May 13, 1975.

component, Persian Gulf imports, the delivery cost of western coal has an exceedingly high transportation component (see Table 3-5). Furthermore, while oil companies frequently own or charter their own vessels, thus bringing these operations in-house, such an option is completely impossible for coal producers in the United States under the law (at least by rail).

The importance of extremely high proportional transportation costs is that it takes away from the coal producer much of the key pricing decision, and puts it in the railroads' hands. Coal's transportation cost—the railroads decision—not its mine mouth cost, becomes the most sensitive variable in eastern and midwestern purchaser's decisions. Thus, even assuming, *in arguendo*, that oil companies could and did "conspiratorially" fix mine mouth coal prices, with the overall rapid increase in importance expected for western coal, this factor becomes of relatively little significance to utility purchasers located in the industrial and population centers east of the Mississippi.

Physical Feasibility

In addition to satisfying the criterion of economic possibility (product substitutability) and the criterion of economic feasibility (profitability), the criterion of physical feasibility must, of course, also be satisfied before coal price stabilization by oil companies becomes a possibility. The previous analyses have basically been sectoral analyses based on generalized data and statistics.

Table 3-5. Approximate Cost Components for Western Coal and Persian Gulf Crude Oil

	Western Coal ($/ton)	Persian Gulf Crude ($/barrel)
F.O.B. Cost	$ 5.00	$12.00
Transportation	15.00	1.50
Total Cost	20.00	13.50
Percent Transportation of Total	75.0%	11.1%

The analyses that follow focus upon the actual circumstances of the individual companies and seek to determine whether noncompetitive pricing actions would be consistent with these circumstances or have been evidenced by their performance. Identification of the factors relevant to individual oil firms with coal production of more than 1 percent of the total market is presented in the order of each company's importance in domestic coal production as measured by national coal market shares.

Continental Oil Company (8.6 Percent Market Share). Basically a western oil company (Continental was the part of the old Standard Oil trust responsible for operations in the Rocky Mountain area), through its Consolidation Coal Company subsidiary, Conoco, owns some of the largest eastern coal reserves in the United States (estimated at 5.4 billion tons). Its eastern thrust is further evidenced by mine development and expansion projects completed and underway in 1975. Of nine such projects, seven were located in states east of the Mississippi.

As a U.S. refiner, Continental is more oriented toward the production of gasoline than it is toward the production of heavy utility fuel oil—the "substitute" for steam coal. As shown in Table 3-6, Conoco sales of residual fuel oil comprise only 10 percent of its total U.S. refined product sales, while gasoline accounts for 52.5 percent of sales.

Conoco acquired Consolidation Coal Company in 1966 when Consolidation's coal production totaled approximately 43 million tons annually. Since the acquisition its coal production has increased to over 50 million tons per year, reaching a high of 58 million tons in 1972. More importantly, its customer mix has increasingly emphasized utility sales every year since its acquisition by Continental, as shown in Table 3-7. In 1965, 61 percent, or approximately 24 million tons, of coal production was sold to

Table 3-6. U.S. Refined Product Sales of Fourteen Selected Major Refiners, 1975 (MB/D)

	Gasoline Sales		Distillates & Other Product Sales		Residual Fuel Oil Sales		Total Product Sales (MB/D)
	MB/D	% of Total	MB/D	% of Total	MB/D	% of Total	
Amerada Hess	202.0	38.6%	Included in gasoline		321.0	61.4%	523.0
Std. Oil of Ohio	216.0	61.7	99.0	28.2%	35.0	10.0	350.0
Exxon	535.3	34.1	625.3	39.8	410.4	26.1	1571.0
Std. Oil of Indiana	570.0	48.9	515.0	44.2	81.0	6.9	1166.0
Shell	524.0	58.0	364.0	38.3	63.9	6.6	951.0
Gulf	467.9	58.8	263.8	33.2	64.0	8.0	795.7
ARCO	327.3	49.6	283.8	43.0	49.3	7.5	660.4
Sun	318.6	46.3	285.0	41.5	83.7	12.2	687.3
Union	248.2	51.4	197.7	40.9	37.3	7.7	483.2
Phillips	304.0	54.8	220.0	39.6	31.0	5.6	555.0
Ashland	63.9	52.9	44.3	36.7	12.6	10.4	120.8
Continental	199.0	52.5	142.0	37.5	38.0	10.0	379.0
Cities Service[a]	165.0	45.5	171.7	47.4	25.8	7.1	362.5
Getty	110.3	39.4	140.0	50.0	29.6	10.6	279.9

[a]"Other Product" sales have been included in the "Residual Fuel Oil" class.

Source: Annual reports, and 10-K Reports, domestic information on Texaco, SOCAL & Mobil not available.

Table 3-7. Consolidation Coal Sales and End Use, 1965-1973

| Year | Production (thousands of tons) | End Use | | |
		Utilities	Industrial	Metallurgical
1965	40,222	61%	21%	18%
1966	43,000	66	19	15
1967	48,699	69	18	13
1968	51,918	71	16	13
1969	53,637	73	16	12
1970	57,365	73	12	15
1971	49,021	76	10	14
1972	58,507	78	9	12
1973	54,421	79	9	12

Source: Conoco annual reports and 10-K reports

utilities, whereas by 1973, 79 percent of its increased coal production, or about 44 million tons of coal, was sold to the utility market. This trend is inconsistent with what one would expect had Consolidation, the largest coal operating company owned by a petroleum company, been avoiding competition with petroleum firms for utility fuel business.

Occidental Petroleum Company (3.5 Percent Market Share). Occidental, the sole owner of Island Creek Coal Company, is the third largest U.S. coal producer. Although incorporated in the United States, Occidental is basically an overseas oil company. Its domestic oil output averaged only 7,200 barrels per day in 1975, and it had no domestic refining or marketing operations. There is therefore no relevant comparison of the relative size and importance of Occidental's U.S. oil and coal operations. In view of its large eastern coal reserves and virtually no petroleum reserves, Occidental has every economic incentive to act competitively with anyone in the pricing and marketing of its coal.

Ashland Oil (2.3 Percent Market Share). Approximately 6 years ago, Ashland entered the coal business by organizing Arch Mineral Corporation. Ashland's current ownership interest in Arch is 48.9 percent. Since 1969, Arch has become one of the country's leading coal producers (ranked number 8), with production of over 14 million tons in 1974. Unlike many other companies in the coal industry, however, Arch is currently producing from *all* of its reserves and has a very weak forward coal reserve picture. While Arch is primarily a western coal producer, the parent company is primarily a midwestern and southern marketer/refiner, with relatively small crude oil production (42,000 barrels a day in 1975). Given Ashland's geographic distribution, and given the fact that, far from sitting on its reserves, it is actually developing reserves owned by others (which cannot be developed by them due to federal legislation), it hardly seems creditable that Ashland would forego coal sales to strengthen the price of fuel oil.

Standard Oil Company of Ohio (1.6 Percent Market Share). Sohio, traditionally the most crude-short of any oil company usually given the title "major," is the owner of the Old Ben Coal Company which, with production of 9.5 million tons in 1974, ranked tenth in the U.S. coal industry. Sohio has marketing and refining operations in the state of Ohio under its own brand and in the Northeast through its BP oil subsidiary. Old Ben has reserves in active mining operations in Illinois, Virginia, and Indiana. Sohio, unlike the other companies covered, has overlapping marketing areas for oil and coal. However, Sohio, with only approximately 10 percent of its total petroleum products sold consisting of residual fuel oil, can hardly be considered a substantial competitor to its Old Ben subsidiary.[a]

Gulf Oil (1.3 Percent Market Share). Gulf Oil Company grew up around production centered in Texas and Oklahoma and marketing operations in the East and Midwest. Its major refineries are located in Texas, Pennsylvania, and Ohio. Since its acquisition of Pittsburgh and Midway Coal Company in 1963, Gulf has been marketing coal in the East and Midwest. However, its plans for Midway, as indicated by its undeveloped resources, are aimed at expansion in the western areas of the country. These undeveloped resources consist of deposits in Colorado, Kansas, Kentucky, and the Powder River Basin area of Wyoming. Gulf, like a number of other oil companies that have become active in the development of steam coal reserves, does not emphasize its production of residual fuel oil in the United States. This can best be illustrated by comparing Gulf's U.S. and foreign refined products sales. As may be seen from Table 3-8, in the United

[a]In 1975, of the 351,000 barrels a day of petroleum products sold, residual fuel oil accounted for 35,000 barrels a day; in 1974, of 333,000 barrels a day residuals accounted for 29,000 barrels. In comparison, Amerada Hess in 1975 refined 523,000 barrels per day, of which its residual fuel oil comprised 299,000 barrels. In 1974, it refined 591,000 barrels per day, of which residual fuel oils accounted for 338,000 barrels.

Table 3-8. **Gulf Oil Company, U.S. and Foreign Refined Products
Sales, 1975**

Product	U.S.		Foreign	
	(MB/D)	*Percent*	*(MB/D)*	*Percent*
Motor Gasoline	467.9	58.8	195.6	24.3
Distillates	208.7	26.2	249.8	31.1
Residual Fuel Oil	64.0	8.0	256.5	31.9
Kerosene	39.8	5.0	25.6	3.2
Other	15.3	1.9	77.0	9.6
Total	795.7	100.0	804.5	100.0

Source: 1975 Gulf Oil Company Annual Report.

States, where Gulf emphasizes gasoline production, it sells only 8 percent of its refined products in the form of residual fuel oil. In Europe just the opposite is the case, with Gulf selling 32 percent of its volume as residual fuel oil.

In summary, even if one accepts that oil and coal are potential competitive energy sources, there is little reason to anticipate the creation of energy monopolies. As Gordon states:

> In no case are both the oil and the coal company large enough to be considered even possibly dominant firms. . . . Moreover, an examination of regional details tends to reinforce the argument. The strongest center of coal-oil competition is the U.S. East Coast, and the only oil company—Continental—owning a major eastern coal producer—Consolidation—does not market oil in the East.[21]

Conclusion

From the preceding it is obvious that neither the economic incentive nor the physical means exist for individual companies to substitute a petroleum-based utility fuel for a coal-based fuel. Further, even in aggregate, an economic basis for such behavior on the part of all petroleum companies (assuming joint profit maximization behavior) does not exist, either at present or in the foreseeable future. Lastly, even if the economic and physical feasibility did exist, and one did believe in the "conspiracy" theory of oil company behavior, the difficulty of short-term substitutability of such fuels is so great as to effectively prevent any fuel "switching" except, possibly, under conditions of the grossest of price disparities. This obviates any need for petroelum companies to maintain coal prices to avoid undercutting utility fuel oil prices.

Because of the preponderance of evidence already cited, therefore, it must be concluded that it is consistent with the best economic interests of petroleum firms active in the coal industry to price independently and competitively. The inclusion of these firms strengthens competition in the coal industry by increasing the number of active and interested parties competing for business. The enactment of legislative barriers to entry applicable to this type of competitor would effectively diminish price competition over what would exist without such restrictions.

THE FINANCING OF NONPETROLEUM ENERGY RESOURCE DEVELOPMENT

It is impossible to predict with great certainty the financial requirements for energy resource development over the next 10 or 15 years. Imponderables affecting such a forecast include the real economic growth rate, the rate of inflation, the degree of energy independence to be achieved, and the course of oil and gas prices (both domestic and imported, controlled and noncontrolled). One thing is certain, however. Whatever the exact magnitude of capital investment required in the nonpetroleum energy resource field in the future, it will be huge compared to previous expenditures by the industry and very significant in relation to capital investment by the private sector of the economy as a whole.

Capital availability over the next decade remains a much-discussed and disputed topic. Various scenarios of capital "sufficiency" or "shortage" have been advanced with differing probabilities attached to each. While the various forecasts do not reach a consensus, one must conclude that there is at least an appreciable chance of capital availability constraining investment decisions over the intermediate term. Accordingly, given current estimates of specific large capital requirements and the possibility of capital-availability constraints, it follows that if development of nonpetroleum energy resources is to receive priority as a goal of national policy, it will be necessary for this industry to be open to as many sources of investment capital as possible. Because petroleum industry capital investment (and thus availability) has historically dwarfed other segments of U.S. manufacturing, to foreclose this source of capital funds—given the possibility of capital constraints in the economy—could have severe adverse effects on the development of nonpetroleum energy resources.

Capital Requirements for Nonpetroleum
Energy Resource Recovery

Three scenarios were examined regarding nonpetroleum energy resource requirements. This analysis leans heavily on work of a similar nature already performed by the Bankers Trust Company[22] as validated by other existing work in the field, and on original research, especially in the nuclear-fuel-cycle area. The three cases examined were:

Case 1—Capital requirements assuming oil imports continuation.
Case 2—Capital requirements assuming oil imports eliminated by 1990.
Case 3—Capital requirements assuming oil imports eliminated by 1985.

In order to project capital requirements, it was necessary to project energy demand. This was done on a sectoral basis. The figures used are quite conservative in light of actual historic figures (see Table 3-9).

Consequently, the projected capital requirements may also have a conservative bias. The sectoral growth rates in Table 3-9 yield the total U.S. energy requirements set forth in Table 3-10, and these, in turn, provide a basis for the breakdown by energy sources.[23]

The allocation of energy resources by sector used in this study is quite similar to that used by the Federal Energy Administration in their *1976 National Energy Outlook*, as shown in Table 3-11. It is important to note that the following analysis (Case 1) assumes that by 1990, nuclear power will provide almost 50 percent of the electrical power-generation base of the United States. This projection could, of course, change radically if new regulatory or legislative constraints are imposed.

From a capital requirements standpoint, however, what is important is not the exact split of energy by source, but rather the fact that if one resource option is foreclosed (that is, nuclear), then investment must be expanded in the others to make up the difference. Because all are relatively capital intensive, our capital

Table 3-9. Historic and Projected Energy Demand Growth, by Sector

Sector	Historic Annual Growth	Projected Annual Growth
Household/Commercial	3%	1.5%
Industrial	3% in 1960s 2% in 1970s	0.6-0.7%
Transportation	3.5% in 1960s 4% in 1970s	2.5%
Electrical Generation	7%	6%

Source: Bankers Trust Company, "Capital Resources for Energy through the Year 1990," New York, 1976.

Table 3-10. Projected U.S. Annual Energy Requirements and Contributions, by Energy Sector (quadrillion BTUs)

	1974	1980	1985	1990
Coal	13.2	18.1	22.4	29.4
Oil	33.5	39.9	42.0	40.5
Gas	22.0	20.5	19.7	19.2
Nuclear	1.2	5.0	12.2	23.8
Hydro Power	3.0	3.3	3.8	4.3
Shale	—	0.1	1.4	4.2
Solar, Geothermal, etc.	—	0.1	0.3	0.7
Total Energy Necessary	72.9	87.0	101.8	122.1
Less Synthetic Fuel Conversion Losses	—	(0.2)	(0.9)	(3.5)
Projected Net Energy Requirements	72.9	86.8	100.9	118.6

requirements projections should be of at least the right order of magnitude even if the resource utilization projection is uncertain.[b] This hypothesis has been validated, as will be shown later, by comparing our projections with those made independently by other studies. All show similar capital needs for nonpetroleum energy resource capital expenditures, despite varying assumptions as to the mix of fuels.

It should be noted that the unit capital costs set forth in Table 3-12 exclude any capital reinvestments that may be necessary to keep facilities running after they have commenced operation. These costs cannot currently be reliably estimated for all energy resource areas, but may be quite significant. For example, the Bureau of Mines estimates that an approximately 1 million ton per year underground coal mine requiring an initial capital investment of $26.5 million will also require deferred capital spending of $11.94 million or about 41 percent again of the initial capital investment.[24] To make some allowance for these costs, where at least their order of magnitude can be projected, we have added 30 percent to the total initial coal capital investment requirement to allow for sustaining necessary capital reinvestments.

In converting BTU requirements to specific energy sources we have used approximately the same BTU conversion factors as those appearing in the FTC Staff Report. Unit capital costs used for non-petroleum energy resource development were as follows:

[b]Indeed, projecting nuclear to attain 50 percent of the electrical power-generation base is a conservative assumption for the purposes of our study because development of alternative resources (coal and synthetics) is actually somewhat more capital intensive than the nuclear-fuel cycle on a dollars-per-BTU basis.

Table 3-11. Energy Demand by Sector, 1985 (quadrillion BTUs)

FEA Projections	Coal	Oil	Gas	Nuclear	Other	Total
Household & Commercial	0.1	8.2	6.4	–	–	14.8
Industrial	4.8	8.2	14.0	–	–	27.1
Transportation	–	22.4	0.8	–	–	23.2
Electrical Generation	15.4	2.7	3.1	8.7	3.9	33.7
Other	0.3	–	(0.2)	–	–	–
Totals	20.6	41.5	24.1	8.7	3.9	98.9
This Study Projections						
Household Commercial	0.1	7.7	9.4	–	0.1	17.3
Industrial	5.8	8.3	8.6	–	–	22.7
Transportation	–	23.4	0.6	–	–	24.0
Electrical Generation	15.3	3.3	2.1	12.2	4.0	36.9
Other	–	–	–	–	–	–
Totals	21.2	42.7	20.7	12.2	4.1	100.9

Source: FEA, "1976 National Energy Outlook," FEA-N-75/713, p. 16; and Banker's Trust Company, "Capital Resources for Energy through the Year 1990," New York, 1976, p. 9.

Coal: $25/ton new capacity for deep mines; $12/ton new capacity for surface mines (including surface reclamation).

Synthetic Gas from Coal: $875 million for typical 250 MMCFPD plant.

Synthetic Crude from Shale: $12 billion for a typical 100,000 BPD plant.

Synthetic Crude from Coal: Assumed equivalent to the cost of syncrude from shale less coal mining costs (or $9,500 per BPD).

Nuclear: $63.5 million for all fuel-cycle facilities necessary to support a 1,000 Mwe nuclear power plant.

These are relatively conservative assumptions in comparison with those made in other studies of the subject, as shown in Table 3-12.

Case 1—Capital Requirements Assuming Oil Import Continuation. Energy sources consistent with this scenario appear in Table 3-13. Netting out the import data from the resources demand data shown in Table 3-14 yields domestic production requirements. Applying the capital investment conversion factors previously described results in the capital investment projection for Case 1, as shown in Table 3-14.

Table 3-12.   Estimated Per Unit Capital Requirements for Recovery of Selected Energy Resources (1975 dollars)

	FEA[a]	Bankers Trust[b]	Continental Illinois Bank[c]	C.F. Braun & Co.[d]	American Petroleum Institute[e]	Actual Developmental Projects[f]	This Study	Units
Coal Gasification	–	2,500	–	3,480–6,000	4,000	3,410–4,000	2,500	$per MCFPD
Shale Oil	6,600[g]	10,000	–	–	20,000	12,000–24,640	12,000	$ per BPD
Coal Liquefaction	–	7,500	–	–	20,000	–	9,500	$ per BPD
Nuclear Fuel Cycle	–	45.3	–	–	–	–	63.5	$ per 1,000 Mwe generating plant
Coal Mining—Deep	39.6	25.0	25.0	–	35.0	–	25.0	$ annual ton
Coal Mining—Strip	21.5	12.0	12.0	–	12.0	–	12.0	$ annual ton

[a]Federal Energy Administration, 1976 National Energy Outlook.

[b]Bankers Trust Co., Capital Resources for Energy through the Year 1990, New York, 1976, expressed in 1974 dollars. Bankers Trust estimates that inflation would have increased their figures by 9 to 10 percent between 1974 and 1975.

[c]"Financing New Coal Mine Development in the Decade Ahead," paper given by Wallace W. Wilson, V.P., Continental Illinois Bank and Trust Co. of Chicago, before the 1976 Financial Conference of the American Mining Conference, April 9, 1976.

[d]"Preliminary Economic Comparison of Six Processes for Pipeline Gas from Coal," presentation to the Eighth Synthetic Pipeline Gas Symposium, October 18, 1976, by C.F. Braun and Co., Evaluation Contractor for the joint ERDA-A.G.A. Coal Gasification Program.

[e]"Investment Requirements for Coal, Synthetic Fuels, Uranium," Staff working paper, American Petroleum Institute, July 16, 1976.

[f]Synthetic Fuels: Quarterly Report, March 1976. Cameron Engineers Inc. presents project-by-project capital estimates for on-going development efforts. The data shown cover the range of estimates shown therein.

[g]Federal Energy Administration, Potential Future Role of Oil Shale—Prospects and Constraints, Washington, D.C., 1974.

Table 3-13. Case 1—Energy Sources (quadrillion BTUs)

Source	1974	1980	1985	1990
Domestic Supply	60.8	71.3	85.9	109.0
Net Imports:				
Oil	12.4	15.7	16.0	13.1
Gas	0.9	2.0	2.2	2.7
Coal	(1.7)	(2.0)	(2.3)	(2.7)
Total	72.9	87.0	101.8	122.1
Net Imports as % of Total	16.6%	18.0%	15.6%	10.8%

Case 2—Capital Requirements Assuming Petroleum Imports Eliminated by 1990. In Case 2 the following assumptions were revised vis-à-vis those used for Case 1:

a. Coal output is projected to be 25% greater by 1990 than was the situation in Case 1.
b. Sixty percent of the incremental coal output is used as a feedstock to manufacture synthetic gas. The remainder is used to manufacture synthetic crude.
c. All gas imports projected for Case 1 are replaced by synthetic gas manufactured from coal by 1990.
d. All oil imports projected in Case 1 are replaced by 1990 with synthetic oil. Most of this synthetic oil is assumed to be manufactured from shale, and the remainder to be derived from coal-based synthetic crude plants and as a by-product of the coal gasification process.

The nonpetroleum capital investment projection for energy resources under these revised assumptions for Case 2 is shown in Table 3-15.

Table 3-14. Case 1—Capital Investment Requirements (billions of 1975 dollars)

	1975-1980	1975-1985	1975-1990
Coal[a]	7.0	14.8	25.5
Synthetic Fuels	2.8	15.4	44.7
Nuclear Fuel Cycle	4.4	9.7	18.6
Total Nonpetroleum Energy	14.2	39.9	88.8

[a]Does not include additional capital expenditure necessary for coal transportation. It has been estimated that such expenditures will be between $12.5 and $20 billion dollars by 1990.

Table 3-15.   Case 2—Capital Investment Requirements (billions of 1975 dollars)

	1975-1980	*1975-1985*	*1975-1990*
Coal[a]	8.5	17.8	32.5
Synthetic Fuels	10.2	62.5	161.7
Nuclear Fuels	4.4	9.7	18.6
	23.1	90.0	212.8

[a]Does not include additional transportation capital investments.

As the United States drives for energy independence, the capital cost is high. Assuming basically fixed oil and gas development, to reach independence by 1990 through alternative energy fuel development would cost on the order of $213 billion, versus the $89 billion for the Case 1 scenario—an increase of 139 percent. Even by 1985, for the Case 2 scenario, capital costs on the order of $90 billion will be incurred, versus $40 billion for Case 1.

Case 3—Capital Requirements Assuming Petroleum Imports Eliminated by 1985. In the Case 3 scenario the assumptions used in Case 1 are revised as follows:

a. Coal output by 1985 will be increased to meet the manufacture of synthetic gas necessary to replace gas imports. This estimated increase in production is approximately 17 percent greater in 1985 than the level assumed in Case 1.
b. All gas imports projected for Case 1 will be replaced by 1985 with synthetic gas manufactured from coal.
c. All petroleum imports projected for Case 1 will be replaced by 1985, primarily with shale oil, and the remainder with liquid petroleum by-products from the synthetic gas process.
d. Environmental restrictions are eased permitting the physical possibility of satisfying assumptions a, b, and c, above.

Under these assumptions, the projection of nonpetroleum energy resource capital costs would be those appearing in Table 3-16.

Under Case 3 assumptions, even by 1980, nonpetroleum capital cost will run approximately $43 billion versus $23 billion projected for Case 2 and the $14 billion for Case 1. By 1985, to reach energy independence we must spend $187 billion on nonpetroleum energy resources for capital investment, versus $90 billion in Case 2 and $40 billion in Case 1. These data, of course, are based upon the simple

Table 3-16. Case 3—Capital Investment Requirements (billions of 1975 dollars

	1975-1980	1975-1985
Coal	8.5	18.9
Synthetic Fuels	30.4	158.6
Nuclear-Fuel Cycle	4.4	9.7
	43.3	187.2

model already described and are obviously subject to numerous qualifications. However, the value of the data is not so much in the absolute dollar figures but in their relative magnitude. In order to determine the confidence we may put in these relative magnitudes we have compared them with those reached by others who have studied the issue (see Table 3-17). It will be noted that while the results of the various studies naturally differ significantly in dollar amounts, it is obvious that *minimum* capital expenditures in the range of $40 to $50 billion (in 1975 dollars) must be made over the next ten years to develop nonpetroleum energy resources. Even these expenditures will not be nearly sufficient to buy energy independence.

Projected Availability of Capital Funds

A few years ago, widespread concern arose over the possibility of a capital shortage in U.S. financial markets. With a long list of investment requirements and price inflation rendering each item on the list more expensive each year, the prospects for adequate capital in the medium term seemed unlikely. A few worried observers of the economy even dared to project a long-term, perhaps even permanent, capital decline. They claimed that balance-of-payment deficits, a contracted labor market, and a dwindling supply of natural resources are all contributing to the greatest erosion of capital the United States has ever experienced.[25]

During the 1974/75 recession, the focus of this problem shifted from financing business investment to financing the rapidly growing federal deficit resulting from a decline in tax revenues and a stimulative fiscal policy. More recently, however, with the economy recovering, concern is again centered on whether enough capital will be available to finance corporate investment requirements in the next decade. The challenges facing corporate investment in general, and the energy industry's expanding needs in particular, is clearly stated in the conclusion of a recent article by Benjamin M. Friedman, a Harvard economist:

Table 3-17.   Estimated Capital Requirements for Recovery of Selected Energy Resources, 1975-1984 (billions of 1975 dollars)

	FEA[a]	Bankers Trust[b]	Continental Illinois Bank[c]	American Petroleum Institute[d]	NEA[e]	This Study
Synthetic Fuels	19.0-22.0	14.0-50.0	N/A	40.0-50.0	22.0	15.4-62.5
Nuclear-Fuel Cycle	7.3	7.7	N/A	N/A	20.8	9.7
Coal Mining[f]	17.7-22.4	12.5-15.0	20.0-21.0	N/A	N/A	14.8-17.8
	44.0-51.7	34.2-72.7	N/A	N/A	N/A	39.9-90.0[g]

[a]Federal Energy Administration, *1976 National Energy Outlook.*

[b]Bankers Trust Co., "Capital Resources for Energy through the Year 1990," New York, 1976. (An inflation factor of 9.5 percent has been applied to the original Bankers Trust data, which was expressed in 1974 dollars.)

[c]"Financing New Coal Mine Development in the Decade Ahead," paper given by Wallace W. Wilson, V.P., Continental Illinois Bank and Trust Co. of Chicago, before the 1976 Financial Conference of the American Mining Conference, April 9, 1976. (1976-1985 data)

[d]"Investment Requirements for Coal, Synthetic Fuels, Uranium," staff working paper, American Petroleum Institute, July 16, 1976. (1976-1985 data)

[e]National Academy of Engineering, *U.S. Energy Prospects: An Engineering Viewpoint,* Washington, D.C., 1974.

[f]Excludes associated transportation costs estimated at an additional $12-20 billion.

[g]Cases I and II only.

The weakness of U.S. fixed investment in 1975 is very likely to prove temporary. After the recession, the amount of fixed investment in the U.S. economy will rise, both absolutely and as a fraction of total economic activity, and so the relevant financial markets will have to expand as well. Financing this fixed investment, a task which must combine a *redirection* of financial flows with an *expansion* of total flows, will be the major problem confronting the money and capital markets. As business undertakes more investment in the aggregate, any individual investment project will have to face increasingly severe competition for financing, since the financial markets' expansion at the margin will be due not to an oversupply of funds but to the pressure of demand for funds for fixed investment purposes.[26]

The range of probable corporate external needs can be expressed in three scenarios describing the total amount of corporate investment in new plant and equipment and the extent to which that investment is financed internally. These scenarios present drastically different assessments of the potential requirements for external funds.[27]

The first scenario assumes high investment and depressed internal funds. In this situation, plant and equipment spending climbs to historically high levels and the recent problems of corporations experiencing declining returns on their existing assets continue, so that retained earnings and internal cash flows remain depressed. The trends of the last several credit cycles toward expanding corporate financial needs and contracting internally generated funds continue under these assumptions. All these factors suggest a future economy that expands rather rapidly and is beset with continuing inflation and depressed corporate profits.

Scenario two includes high investment with moderate generation of internal funds. In this case, plant and equipment spending climbs to the same historical high levels assumed in the first scenario, but corporate retained earnings and internal funds expand and rebound to the same average fraction of GNP they attained in the 1950s and early 1960s. Under these conditions, a substantial fraction of corporate investment is financed internally. The economy expands without the intense inflationary pressure of the recent years, and corporations are able to maintain increased profit margins.

The third scenario assumes moderate investment and moderate generation of internal funds. Plant and equipment investment declines in this case from recent levels to a new level similar to that of the 1950s and early 1960s. At this new level, increases in capital spending would be confined to several categories of investments, such as energy development, pollution control, and capacity additions within some of the basic materials industries. Most other capital spending would decrease. With corporate retained earnings and internal funds rebounding to the average levels they attained in the 1950s and early 1960s, external funding requirements are reduced. This suggests a future economy that expands slowly with lower inflationary pressures, and in which corporate investments in productive capacity are made only after increased returns on existing capacity are realized.

Because corporate and governmental financial needs must be supplied by private savings, the savings behavior of households in an important determinant of the capacity of the financial system to fund them. Data from the last five credit cycles (from 1954 through 1974) suggest that the rate of net household savings[c] has fluctuated between 5.4 and 6.6 percent of GNP.

Figure 3-1 shows the magnitude of corporate external financing requirements under the three scenarios described above in relation to net household savings at 6 percent of GNP. As would be expected,

---

[c]Net household savings is defined as the sum of accumulated net financial investment (assets minus liabilities) plus the net increase in residential construction (the dollar value of new home purchases minus depreciation from the existing housing stock).

Figure 3-1. Illustration of Corporate Net External Funds Required as Percent of Net Savings in the Household Sector

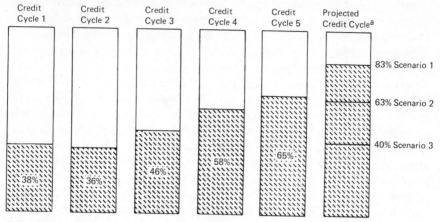

aHousehold net savings rate is assumed to be 6 percent, as a percent of GNP.

Key:
☐ Government Financing and New Home Construction
▨ Corporate Net External Funds Required

Source: Environmental Protection Agency, *Economic and Financial Impacts of Federal Air and Water Pollution Control on the Electric Utility Industry*, May 1976.

scenario 1 requires a much higher ratio of corporate external funds to net savings than has ever existed. Thus if scenario 1 occurs, there will almost certainly be a substantial capital shortage, causing the "crowding out" from capital markets of weaker corporations and industries. Under scenario 2, the external needs of corporations could probably be financed along with new housing and state and local government projects, as long as the federal government does not generate a substantial deficit. This is about the equivalent of the tightest conditions experienced since 1954. If scenario 3 occurs, corporate external needs should be easily financed, leaving substantial funds available for other uses and investments in the economy.

Naturally everyone must attach one's own probability assessments to the three scenarios described. From most prospectives, however, it is likely that the occurrence of scenario 1, with concurrent capital constraints, must be accorded at least an appreciable possibility. Recent studies in this field reflect this uncertainty:

Some recent long-run studies of capital adequacy for the 1975-1985 period have concluded that adequate capital will be available without a major distortion of savings and interest rate patterns. Others suggest that there is substantial risk that capital demands will outstrip supply at reasonable rates by a wide enough margin to cause serious difficulties.[28]

A summary of the results of five of these studies is as follows:[29]

1. New York Stock Exchange	Savings level inadequate to meet investment demand by $520 billion in 1974-1985.
2. The Brookings Institute	Financing capital needs not "unmanageable." Further shifts to debt financing.
3. Data Resources, Inc.	1. Shortages of physical capacity not likely.
	2. Financing of capital outlays is relatively easy until 1980 with slight tightness in 1976/77.
	3. Financing becomes more difficult after 1980, especially 1981 and 1984.
	4. Ratios of short-term to long-term liabilities and debt-equity rise, causing some cutbacks in investment.
4. Labor Department	Adequate funds for investment; 4-5 percent unemployment. Further shift in balance sheet structure as between debt and equity toward higher debt proportions.
5. Chase Econometrics	1. Recession in 1978 attributed to monetary policy.
	2. Investment curtailed by lack of internal funds, high borrowing costs.

Sources of Capital Funds

It will be noted that even the more optimistic of the foregoing projections foresee a rise in the proportion of corporate debt to equity financing. This brings up the question of the specific sources of capital funds to be invested in nonpetroleum energy resource development.

Hypothetically, any sufficiently attractive investment opportunity should be able to draw on capital resources from all areas of the private sector. In reality, this is not the case. Corporate investors tend to place their capital funds in areas that bear at least some degree of similarity to their original businesses. They do this to reduce risk. Management, already heavily involved in a specific business area, has a greater degree of confidence in its ability to project the future of that area and to manage related businesses. Even where companies deliberately diversify, they often do so to alleviate risk, that is, to invest in certain industries that are either noncyclical or countercyclical to the cycles of their own businesses. Management, however, will take risks (and is in the business of taking risks) where the probable payoffs are projected to be great enough. This means that the economic returns expected from an unknown area must be greater than those projected for a known area (all other factors being equal) to compensate for the greater risk incurred in moving into the unknown field.

Given these considerations, it then is logical to assume that, with no artificial constraints, future nonpetroleum energy resource investments would be made by companies already in the field or having interests closely aligned to the field. Such industries are already represented by a number of the companies having investments in the nonpetroleum resource area. These companies primarily include petroleum, electric utilities, steelmaking, and mining firms. Naturally, funds would also come from independent coal producers. All of these industries share, at least partially, a number of important attributes, including: (1) technological similarity or synergy; (2) high capital intensiveness; and (3) a history of management making long lead-time investments with concurrently extended payback periods. These five industries, then, become the leading candidates for supplying capital funds for investment in the nonpetroleum energy resource field.

Funds to be attracted from outside of these industries would likely require higher prospective returns because of the greater perceived risks by corporate managements unfamiliar with the business. This means that projects that are only marginally attractive by the standards of "primary" investors (that is, the five industries mentioned above) would be unattractive by the standards of other private investors. It in turn follows that should primary investors be constrained from investing in the nonpetroleum energy resource field, investment would be less than it would otherwise be. Development of alternative energy resources would accordingly be diminished. On examination of the five above industries, it becomes readily apparent that petroleum company involvement is necessary if this primary group of corporate investors is to exploit all possible resource developments.

The Electric Utility Industry. The financial situation of the electric utilities has deteriorated substantially in the past decade. The return on equity for this industry dropped during a period in which inflation forced investors to demand increasing returns. Additionally, the quality of the industry's earnings has been declining due to changes in utility accounting procedures (such as the treatment of large construction expenditures for projects not yet completed and producing revenue). Interest rates have risen for utilities while their security issues have been continually downgraded by security-rating firms. Combined with increasing debt/equity ratios, these rates have caused interest coverage to drop close to minimum levels, making it extremely difficult for the industry in general to raise even sufficient capital to cover increased generation requirements. As one large bank stated:

> During 1973 and 1974, the investor owned utility industry was probably pushing at the edge of its capability to raise funds. . . . Probably no industry has come closer to the edge of financial disaster.[30]

With its debt/equity ratio already at a workable maximum and its profits governed by close consumer-sensitive regulation, it is questionable whether electric utilities in the future will have sufficient capital funds to satisfactorily meet their own power-plant investment requirements, much less to invest into integrating backwards into fuel production.[31] Using the three scenarios discussed previously, electric utility external financing requirements for scenarios 2 and 3 are projected to be far above the percentage of all corporate financing they have historically maintained (see Table 3-18). The first scenario describes a capital shortage condition that will cause fierce competition for funds among those corporations competing, so that many electric utilities would be constrained under this scenario, as well.

Steelmakers and Mining Companies. Steel manufacturers and mining companies are both faced with problems similar to those facing utilities, although less severe in magnitude. In both industries there is widespread feeling that financing their own internal expansion plans will be difficult enough without looking for new fields to conquer. As Professor William Hogan, one of the leading steel

Table 3-18.   Investor-Owned Electric Utility: External Financing, Including Pollution Control, 1975-1985 (billions of 1975 dollars)

	1971- 1974	*Scenario 1*	*Scenario 2*	*Scenario 3*
All Non-financial Corporations	$249	$1,041	$789	$484
Electric Utilities	$ 44	$174	$174	$174
Percent of All Corporate Financing	18%	17%	22%	36%
Percent of Net Household Savings	11.5%	14.0%	14.0%	14.3%

Source: *Economic and Financial Impacts of Federal Air and Water Pollution Controls on the Electric Utility Industry* (EPA-230/3-76-013), May 1976.

industry experts, stated in reviewing steel capacity projections for 1980:

> Adequate funding will be difficult. . . . It is evident that companies in the steel industry face a formidable task in the next five years if they are to amass and spend the $5.25 billion needed annually to care for replacement, expansion and pollution control.[32]

Mining companies, according to the *Wall Street Journal* report of June 23, 1976, confronted an almost identical problem:

> According to various estimates, capital outlays of as much as $6 billion will be needed over the next 10 years just to increase domestic copper production to meet rising demand. The copper companies just don't have that sort of money. Frank Miliken, president of Kennecott Copper Corp., says his company ought to be spending half a billion dollars on expansion, but is unable to carry its debt load (which doubled last year) as well as amass large amounts of capital. As a result, Kennecott is deferring its expansion plans.

Interestingly, Kennecott is the current owner of Peabody Coal, the nation's largest coal producer; and is under an FTC order to divest itself of Peabody.

Not only are the needs for capital outlays on steel capacity likely to absorb all of the industry's available funds, the sheer absolute size of energy capital needs makes steelmakers and mining firms unlikely candidates to supply them. Capital expenditures of major steelmakers and mining firms were $3.7 and $3.8 billion, respectively, in

1975.[33] Given annual average requirements of between $4 and $9 billion for alternative resource energy development over the next 10 years, it is evident that even if they had uncommitted funds, they could scarcely make a dent in the capital requirements for nonpetroleum energy development.

Independent Coal Producers. A number of factors weigh heavily against independent coal producers contributing a significant portion of the capital resources necessary to fully develop alternative energy sources. The projected expenditures required for adequate coal mine development alone are immense. The Federal Energy Administration forecasts, in its *1976 National Energy Outlook*, that between $17.7 and $22.4 billion will be necessary to increase coal production over the next ten years. A comparable study by Amex Coal indicates that capital requirements over the same time would range between $15.4 and $16.4 billion, and more recently updated this estimate to $25 billion.[34] The projection used in this study conservatively shows a requirement of between $11.5 and $14.5 billion over the same time frame, excluding any capital reinvestments necessary to keep mines running once they are in operation. In contrast, over the ten-year period 1965-1975 the entire coal industry's capital spending was $6.5 billion, most of which was not spent by independent coal producers but by firms with major interests in other fields. As a point of reference, the five leading independent coal producers in 1975 (Eastern Fuel and Gas Associates, Westmoreland Coal, North American Coal, Peter Kiewit, and Pittston) combined accounted for less than $0.4 billion in coal-oriented capital expenditures for the two-year period 1974-1975. It is evident that independent coal producers cannot begin to generate the capital funds necessary (from traditional capital sources) to develop even a small portion of the coal reserves that energy forecasts indicate should be developed, not to mention investment in alternative energy source fields such as synthetic fuels where they might otherwise be expected to have an interest. As one of the reports to the Energy Policy Project of the Ford Foundation states:

> The late Eli Goldston, Chairman of the Board of Eastern Gas and Fuel Associates, suggested Federal guarantees of coal mine development loans as the only method to permit that industry to raise the billions of dollars it will need.[35]

Petroleum Industry. When we turn to the petroleum industry, however, virtually all the pertinent factors indicate that oil companies are in a unique position to contribute significant capital funds to alternative energy development. Petroleum companies by any standard of measurement are large. They account for five of the top ten corporations appearing on *Fortune*'s list of the five hundred largest industrial companies in the United States; for ten of the largest twenty; for fifteen of the largest fifty; and for twenty of the largest seventy-six. The largest of the twenty petroleum companies had assets in 1975 of $32.8 billion; the smallest of the twenty had $4.2 billion. Oil companies are large because their cumulative capital investment has, by virtue of the nature of their business, been enormous. In the single year 1975, nineteen large oil companies accounted for over $19 billion in new capital expenditures (see Table 3-19). By way of comparison, these expenditures alone amounted to

Table 3-19.   Capital Expenditures by Selected Major Petroleum Companies, 1975[a] (millions of dollars)

Company	Petroleum & Chemical	Nonpetroleum Energy[b]	All Other	Total
Exxon	4,441	79	–	4,520
Texaco	1,637	37[c]	–	1,674
Standard of Indiana	1,858	18[c]	–	1,876
Shell	1,136	31	60	1,227
Gulf	934	125	75	1,131
Mobil	1,435	14[c]	–	1,449
Sun	389	57	91	537
Marathon	360	–	–	360
Cities Service	434[c]	5[c]	–	439
Phillips	729	–	–	729
Socal	1,814	457	–	2,271
Amerada Hess	283	–	–	283
Continental	667	219	2	888
Tenneco	322	–	223	545
Superior	44	16	–	N/A
Louisiana Land	117	–	–	117
Ashland Oil	223	6	36	283
Occidental Petroleum	415	98	–	496
Kerr McKee	177	58	–	235
	17,425	1,220	484	

[a]Data for Sohio, Arco, Union, and Getty not available.
[b]Includes coal, oil shale, synthetic fuels, uranium, geothermal, and all other non-oil energy.
[c]May include some non-energy capital expenses.
Sources: Company annual reports and 10-K Reports.

three times the projected average annual investment of $6.5 billion in nonpetroleum energy sources required over the decade 1976-1986.[36]

The operational aspects of these companies also make them likely candidates to invest in alternative energy sources. Petroleum firms in general have relatively strong balance sheets as measured by their ratio of long-term debt to equity. As may be seen from Table 3-20, the petroleum industry's debt/equity ratio of 0.28 is less than that of most industries and significantly less than that of the average of 0.52 for all industries in the private sector. All other factors being equal, this gives firms within the petroleum industry some flexibility as to the means of their financing in terms of their ability to raise external monies without the generation of matching internal equity.

Funds are generated internally from two sources—net profit after tax and noncash expenses, the largest of which is depreciation. It is important to note that because the asset base of the petroleum industry is so great, their profits, although only average in terms of rate of return on investment (see Table 3-21), are enormous in absolute dollar terms. For example, the five largest petroleum companies in 1975 earned an average rate of return on stockholders' equity of slightly less than 11.8 percent, but their combined net income amounted to $5.6 billion.

The second important source of funds for the petroleum industry is depreciation. Because the petroleum industry has such a high percentage of fixed assets to total assets (see Table 3-22), its

Table 3-20.   1974 Debt-to-Equity Ratio for Selected Major Industries[a]

Drugs	0.19
Petroleum	0.28
Motor Vehicles	0.29
Steel Manufacturers	0.37
Machine Tools	0.39
Textiles	0.39
Computers & Office Equipment	0.41
Cement	0.42
Paper	0.50
Nonferrous Metals	0.57
Aircraft	0.59
Building Materials	0.74
Rubber	0.92
Radio & TV Equipment	1.13

[a]32-industry average = 0.52.

Source: Investors Management Sciences, COMPUSTAT® computer readable data.

Table 3-21. Worldwide   Return   on   Equity   of   Petroleum   Companies, 1965-1974

	Percent Return on Equity	
	All Industry[a]	Petroleum
1965	13.8	11.9
1966	14.1	12.6
1967	12.6	12.9
1968	13.2	12.9
1969	12.7	12.1
1970	10.3	10.9
1971	10.9	11.2
1972	12.1	10.8
1973	14.5	15.6
1974	15.3	19.9
Weighted Average		
1965-1974	13.0	13.4
1965-1972	12.3	11.8

[a]Excludes transportation companies, public utilities, and financial companies.
Source: Citibank (New York).

depreciation as a percent of total assets is correspondingly high. Thus, in both relative and absolute terms, depreciation charges for the petroleum industry are quite large, yielding a significant source of funds to be reinvested.

Other Industries (Nonrelated Investors). While it is of considerable importance that petroleum companies would play a significant role in financing alternative energy source development, their absence could materially affect the total amount of capital available for nonpetroleum resource development from the entire private sector. As the preceding analysis points out, the U.S. petroleum industry, along with investor-owned electric utilities, account for a substantial proportion of total private-sector capital outlays. (The importance of these industry groups in proportion to the U.S. private sector as a whole is highlighted in Table 3-23.) These two industries jointly accounted for 24 percent of all plant and equipment expenditures in the private sector in 1970. Historically, this percentage has been steadily increasing, as illustrated in Table 3-24, and stood in 1974 at 30.5 percent.

Not only is this a large percentage in relation to private-sector capital investments as a whole, but its importance becomes even

Table 3-22. 1974 Fixed-to-Total Assets Ratios for Selected Major Industries[a]

Petroleum	0.79
Cement	0.75
Steel Manufacturers	0.74
Paper	0.71
Nonferrous Metals	0.65
Motor Vehicles	0.46
Computers & Office Equipment	0.45
Building Materials	0.44
Rubber	0.43
Radio & TV Equipment	0.42
Drugs	0.42
Textiles	0.41
Machine Tools	0.29
Aircraft	0.27

[a]32-industry average = 0.51.

Source: Investors Management Sciences, COMPUSTAT® computer readable data base.

more pronounced when compared with other industries (see Table 3-25). There it becomes evident that aside from the communications industry (that is, AT&T) and perhaps chemicals, no one industry, or even small group of nonrelated industries, could hope to contribute a significant proportion of the $4-5 billion annually that will be needed as a minimum to develop nonpetroleum energy resources over the next decade.

ENERGY RESOURCE RESEARCH AND DEVELOPMENT

We have just dealt with the size and risk of capital investments in the development of alternative energy sources, as well as the special ability of the large petroleum companies to undertake such long-term investments. It follows that insight may be gained by analyzing the magnitude, output, focus, and commercialization of R&D efforts.

Before discussing these specific aspects of petroleum companies' R&D activities, we should bear in mind what the economics of industrial organization would lead us to expect. The relationship of market structure and firm size to R&D intensity has long been a matter of considerable interest to economists and public policymakers alike. The hypothesis that market structure affects techno-

Table 3-23.   Importance of Petroleum and Electric Utility Industries in Total Output of the Economy, Aggregate Plant and Equipment Expenditures, and External Capital Markets, 1970

Economy:

Total Receipts of Active Corporations, 1970	$1,751.0 billion
Total Corporate Capital Outlays	$ 79.7 billion
External Capital Raised by Nonfinancial Corporations	$ 39.8 billion

Energy Sectors:	*U.S. Petroleum*	*Investor-Owned Electric Utilities*	*Total*
Sector Recipts (billions of dollars)	62.9[a]	18.8	81.7
Receipts as % of Total Receipts of Active Corporations	3.6	1.1	4.7
Plant and Equipment Expenditures (billions of dollars)	8.2	10.7	18.9
Plant and Equipment Expenditures as % of Corporate Capital Outlays	10.2	13.4	23.6
External Capital Raised (billions of dollars)	1.6[a]	8.2	9.8
External Capital as % of Total Capital Raised by Nonfinancial Corporations	4.0	20.6	24.6

[a]Approximated by adjusting Chase Manhattan Bank's sample of 28 petroleum companies, "Financial Analysis of a Group of Petroleum Companies, 1970." The approximation assumes that Chase's 28-firm sample represents 75 percent of the world petroleum industry and that the U.S. share of that industry's expenditures is 57 percent.

Sources: "Flow of Funds," *Federal Reserve Bulletin*, March 1973, p. A-72; Corporation Income Tax Returns, 1970, Internal Revenue Service, Table A; Edison Electric Institute, *1971 Statistical Yearbook*, Tables 34-S, 50-S, and 56-S; Chase Manhattan Bank, *Capital Investments of the World Petroleum Industry, 1970*, Schedule 1, Net Exploration Expenses: *Survey of Current Business* (various issues).

logical progress dates back to the 1880s. Although many economists have written extensively on this topic, the name of Professor Joseph Schumpeter is most commonly associated with the formulation and development of the hypothesis that only large firms with accumulated surpluses—which by definition meant that these firms were earning above average rates of return—could afford to invest in risky innovational activities. In addition, Schumpeter argued that innovational competition carried on by large firms with some degree of

Table 3-24. New Plant and Equipment Expenditures for Oil, Gas, and Investor-Owned Utility Industries

Year	Oil and Gas[a]	Investor-Owned Electric Utility	Total All Industries	Oil, Gas, and Utility Total to All Industries
1965	$ 6.38 billion	$ 4.43 billion	$ 54.42 billion	19.0%
1966	7.13	5.38	63.51	19.7
1967	7.65	6.75	65.47	22.0
1968	8.35	7.66	67.76	23.6
1969	8.18	8.94	75.56	22.7
1970	8.23	10.65	79.71	23.6
1971	7.26	12.86	81.21	24.8
1972	9.05	14.48	88.44	26.6
1973	10.64	15.94	99.74	26.6
1974	16.63[b]	17.63	112.40	30.5

[a]Does not include lease rentals or geological and geophysical expenses, but does include lease bonus payments.
[b]Preliminary figure.
Sources: New Plant and Equipment Expenditures: *Survey of Current Business* (various issues). Chase Manhattan Bank, *Capital Investments of the World Petroleum Industry*, annual (various issues).

market power, in contrast with that identified in economic textbooks with "perfectly competitive" (atomistic) industries, was the primary source of rising real incomes and living standards. The development of the Schumpeterian hypothesis—that there is a positive relationship between firm size, concentration, and the rate of technological innovation—caused a considerable stir in the economics profession. This hypothesis has been subjected to empirical testing by some dozen or more scholars, and so far none has yielded unambiguous results. However, several generalizations can be made, and the following two statements have been supported by the majority of empirical investigations.

1. If we divide the corporate population into two classes—large firms that for the most part operate in industries having concentration ratios falling within the broad range between the petroleum and motor vehicle industries, and small firms that tend to operate in industries in the lower range of concentration—we find that those in the first group do account for a disproportionately large amount of the business-financed R&D, research personnel employed, or number of patents obtained.

2. Although attempts to determine the relationship between industrial concentration and innovational intensity through the use of

Table 3-25. Capital Expenditures (billions of 1975 dollars)

Industry	1971-1975	1975
Electric Utilities	$77.94 billion	$17.00 billion
Communications	62.21	12.74
Petroleum	35.06	10.51
Chemicals	23.29	6.25
Machinery	18.04	4.50
Food & Beverages	14.86	3.26
Mining	14.29	3.79
Gas Utilities	13.78	3.14
Electrical Machinery	12.65	2.31
Iron and Steel	11.36	3.71
Airlines	10.59	1.84
Railroads	10.52	2.55
Autos, Trucks and Parts	10.39	2.06
Paper and Pulp	10.02	2.95
Fabricated Metals & Instruments	9.48	2.73
Nonferrous Metals	8.54	2.28
Rubber	5.95	1.00
Stone, Clay and Glass	5.75	1.42
Textiles	3.61	.66
Aerospace	3.08	.92

Source: Adapted from data appearing in *Business' Plans for New Plant and Equipment* (New York: McGraw-Hill, 1971-1975).

regression models have not yielded completely unambiguous or conclusive results, in general most of them find at least a weak *positive* correlation between concentration ratios and R&D/sales ratios, although the results vary considerably from one industry to another, with the purity of the data and the particular specifications of the regression model. Scherer, whom we have quoted often before, gives what is perhaps the most reasonable summarization:

> Using one specification of the model, Schumpeter's hypothesis is sustained with flying colors. Using the alternative and theoretically preferred specification, the support is weaker but not entirely absent. . . .
> Technological vigor appears to increase with concentration mainly at the relatively low levels of concentration. When the four-firm concentration ratio exceeds 50% or 55%, additional market power is probably not conducive to more vigorous technological efforts.[37]

In examining the R&D intensity in the petroleum industry we will find that these theoretical generalizations are valid for this industry; the larger petroleum companies do more R&D and the largest eight companies account for a disproportionately large share of research. In other words, there is nothing unusual about the R&D efforts of petroleum companies; they perform as economic theory would predict, given their large size and the relatively moderate rate of concentration in the industry.

Magnitude of R&D

It is useful, initially, for the purpose of understanding the magnitude of the petroleum company's investment in energy R&D efforts, to compare their total expenditures to total industrial expenditures for energy R&D in the years 1972-1974. Table 3-26 indicates that in 1972, 62 percent and in 1973, 55 percent of all private energy R&D was being performed by petroleum companies.

Within the industry itself, there is a tendency for the proportion of R&D to sales revenues to increase with size. This finding from our

Table 3-26. Total Industrial R&D Expenditures for Energy, by Industry, 1972-1974 (millions of dollars)[a]

Industry	1972	1973	1974
Total	$714 million	$1,004 million	$1,197 million
(Federal funds)	(224)	(385)	(479)
(Company funds)	(489)	(619)	(718)
Petroleum refining and extraction	293	313	372
Electrical equipment and communication	193	318	374
Chemicals and allied products	62	58	84
Aircraft and missiles	52	101	129
Scientific and mechanical measuring instruments	13	_[b]	_[b]
Primary metals	10	_[b]	_[b]
Machinery	8	_[b]	_[b]
Nonmanufacturing industries	35	38	50
All other	48	176	188

[a]This includes not only extraction techniques but all phases of energy R&D research efforts (e.g., nuclear reactor development would in large part be funded by those companies included above under "Electrical equipment and communication").

[b]For the years 1973 and 1974, these figures are included in the figures for "All other."

Source: National Science Foundation, *Science Resources Studies-Highlights*, January 14, 1976, (NSF 76/300).

survey is in keeping with what the economics of industrial organization would lead us to expect. Although we are unable to reveal the individual company ratios due to confidentiality, Table 3-27 summarizes the proportion of revenues and energy R&D accounted for by the top eight companies in the years 1971-1975. These data clearly show that the largest companies of the group surveyed invest slightly, but consistently, more R&D dollars (in relation to their size as measured by revenues) than does the group as a whole. Moreover, when individual company data are analyzed over the same period, these findings are further verified.

The results reached in this survey do not differ substantially from those published by the National Science Foundation, even though the latter include all sales and R&D activities of large oil companies. The NSF compilations for 1973 show the ratios of R&D expenditures to sales for the largest four petroleum companies to be 0.8 percent; for the next four largest, 0.7 percent; and for the next twelve largest, 0.5 percent.[38]

Output of R&D

It is difficult to find a single comprehensive statistic for measuring the effectiveness of R&D expenditures. Patents, however, have frequently been used by economists as one such measure. The data from our survey demonstrate that the larger petroleum companies have indeed been effective in converting their R&D expenditures into patents. Table 3-28 presents the statistics for patents obtained by the member companies of the industry.

Focus

It is not enough to show that oil companies indeed perform a large quantity of R&D and that patents result from this R&D. It is also necessary to follow this one step further and try to assess the results in terms of development and commercialization of these patents. Completeness is important in evaluating the effectiveness of the total circle of an R&D process. It should be noted that some divestiture proponents have alleged that the heavy investments being made by petroleum companies in substitute technology are aimed toward discovering technology and patenting it while purposely not developing it. Thus, they argue, other energy source technology is held as insurance for the day when petroleum reserves dry up or to preclude firms outside the petroleum industry from using it.

To systematically relate patents to output is extremely difficult if not impossible since of the thousands of patents registered, many have little or no value in a strict commercial sense, many represent

Table 3-27.   Energy R&D Expenditures and Sales Revenues of 23 Major Oil Companies[a] (millions of dollars)

	1971	1972	1973	1974	1975	Total
Energy R&D Expenditures						
Largest Eight Companies[b]	220	263	294	370	399	1,546
All Companies Surveyed[c]	286	327	362	458	510	1,943
Largest Eight as % of All Co.'s	77%	80%	81%	81%	78%	80%
Sales Revenues						
Largest Eight Companies[b]	48,027	60,183	80,672	140,895	146,011	475,788
All Companies Surveyed	71,690	79,395	106,445	184,498	192,295	634,323
Largest Eight as % of Co.'s	67%	76%	76%	76%	76%	75%

[a]Excludes petro-chemical revenues.

[b]Only six of largest eight companies reported in 1971; only seven in 1972.

[c]Includes three companies reporting *no* R&D expenditures.

Table 3-28.   Petroleum Company Patents and Revenues

	Total Patents 1971-1976[a]	Total Patents Less Petrochemical	Total Sales Revenue 1971-1975 $MM	Total Revenue Less Chemical 1971-1975 $MM
Exxon	1,739	1,141	164,072	153,258
Shell	1,667	1,326	28,989	24,740
Phillips	1,419	692	18,372	14,314
Texaco	1,176	734	77,654	77,457
Mobil	818	528	68,349	65,108
Socal	810	518	56,131	53,690
Gulf	672	490	59,375	n/a
Sunoco	638	448	14,215	14,219
Arco	465	317	26,892	24,969
Conoco	427	353	26,521	25,029
Amoco	396	291	38,212	34,047
Cities Service	271	193	11,714	11,192
Union	262	149	18,048	16,707
Sohio	196	182	8,816	7,816
Marathon	156	109	10,998	10,998
Ashland	131	97	13,663	11,279
Occidental	26	10	18,560	12,677
Kerr-McGee	1	−	5,360	3,948
Commonwealth	1	−	2,915	2,915
Getty	−	−	10,890	10,890
Quaker State	−	−	1,069	1,069
Murphy	−	−	3,051	3,051
Amerada Hess	−	−	11,494	11,494

[a]Through June 1976.

Source: API Abstracting Service.

minor modifications to existing processes, and in some cases the economics of development do not justify the investment. In the course of this study, however, two simple patent searches were performed in conjunction with a search of the literature about commercial and development projects in the area of coal conversion and oil shale technology.[d]   A summary of these research results appears in Tables 3-29 through 3-31, which indicate that where the development of technological advances has been economically feasible, oil companies tend to move from the patent stage to commercialization and licensing.

[d]The complete patent searches and descriptions of these projects appear in Appendices A and D, respectively.

Table 3-29. Coal Conversion Patents by Type of Company, 1964-1975

Type of Company	*Total Number of Patents*	*Percent of Total*	*Number of Companies*	*Total Number of Claims*[a]	*Percent of Total*
Petroleum Companies	29	46.0%	8	344	53.6%
Process Contractors & Engineering Companies	18	28.5	3	165	25.9
Associations, Institutes, Research Organizations	3	4.7	1	21	3.2
Coal Companies[b]	6	9.5	2	40	6.2
U.S. Government	5	7.9	N/A	58	9.0
Unclassified Companies	2	3.2	2	14	2.1
Total	63	100.0	17	642	100.0

[a]The number of claims refers to the number of individual processes or parts involved in a patent.

[b]Of the six patents granted to coal companies, three were granted to Consolidation Coal after its acquisition by CONOCO.

Source: Cameron Engineers, *Synthetic Fuels* and *Oil Shale and Related Fuels, 1964-1975*; U.S. Patent Office, Class 201 (subclasses 25 and 35); Class 48 (subclass 210); Class 208 (subclasses 8 and 9).

Table 3-29 shows the coal-conversion patent summary from 1964 to 1976, while Table 3-30 is a summary of oil shale patents. A comparison of the petroleum companies holding coal-conversion patents with the lists of petroleum companies holding substantial coal reserves shows that the eight petroleum companies that account for 54 percent of these claims all have sizable investments in coal reserves. Likewise, of the eighteen petroleum companies holding patents on oil shale, thirteen not only own oil shale reserves but either have commercial or demonstration projects on line or in the planning stages.

Table 3-31 shows oil shale patents by companies and also lists the numbers of projects in which these individual companies are presently involved. Of the companies holding patents in oil shale, 18 of the 31 (58 percent; see Table 3-30) are petroleum companies. Of the 86 patents included in the patent search, at least 24 appear to have resulted in some type of project. Nine have been classified as commercial, as determined by the size of the investment or the potential for actually putting on line a plant that would be commercially viable. The estimated costs of such projects are anywhere from $500 million to $1.5 billion. While non-oil companies are heavily involved in 11 of the 15 demonstration projects, all of the commercial projects are funded entirely by oil companies.

Table 3-30. Oil Shale Patents by Type of Company, 1964-1975

Type of Company	Total Number of Patents		Number of Companies	Total Number of Claims[a]	
		Percent of Total			Percent of Total
Petroleum Companies	69	80.2%	18	656	78.2%
Manufacturing & Engineering Companies	8	9.3	6	85	10.1
Associations, Institutes, Research Organizations	6	7.0	4	62	7.4
Unclassified Companies	3	3.5	3	36	4.3
Total	86	100.0	31	839	100.0

[a]The number of claims refers to the number of individual processes or parts involved in a patent.

Source: Cameron Engineers, *Synthetic Fuels* and *Oil Shale and Related Fuels, 1964-1975*; U.S. Patent Office, Class 201 (subclasses 25 and 35); Class 48 (subclass 210); Class 208 (subclasses 8 and 9).

Many of the demonstration processes involving non-oil company participants also have as partners the Bureau of the Mines, NSF, or ERDA, and are focused in areas that petroleum companies would not find commercially attractive to them, either because of a lack of markets or lack of compatibility with refining or transportation facilities already on line. For example, for oil shale the petroleum companies seem to hold patents dealing with the surveying, recovering, and retorting of oil from shale; the Institute of Gas Technology and the American Gas Association hold patents for gasification of the oil recovered from shale; and the process contractors in engineering firms hold patents directly relating to pipelining, conversion techniques, retorting apparati, and the like. These patents and their development are reflected in the demonstration projects, which are small in scale, low in price, and focus on business areas in which the nonpetroleum companies are normally engaged.

As to the petroleum companies, the conclusion one can draw from this analysis is that their patents, the result of focused research, reflect the realities of well-defined business strategies of diversification in the technologies that are most in synchronization with either the way they do business—their markets and technology—or represent their present plans for future diversification.

Table 3-31. Oil Shale Patent Holders, Participants in Commercial or Demonstration Projects (as of March 1976)

Company	Oil Shale (# Patents)	Participants (# Projects)
Union	2	3
Arco	10	4
Ashland	–	1
Tosco	7	2
Shell	5	2
Amoco	1	4
Gulf	–	4
Sun	1	2
Phillips	6	4
Paraho[a]	2	2
Institute of Gas Technology	1	1
Occidental	–	1
Dow Chemical	–	1
Superior Oil	–	1
Sohio	1	1
Bureau of Mines	–	3
Nat'l Science Foundation	–	2

[a]Consortium of: A.G. McGee, Arco, Carter, Chevron, Cleveland Cliffs, Gulf, Kerr-McGee, Marathon, Mobil, Phillips, Shell, Sohio, Southern California Edison, Amoco, Texaco, and Webb Resources.

Source: Cameron Engineers, *Synthetic Fuels* (March 1976).

Commercialization/Licensing

The next stage in the research/development/commercialization/transfer chain covered in this study is that of licensing—the revenues from which provide an incentive for rapid process development. To the question on the survey about licensing policies, the overwhelming response is that all technology is licensed on a nondiscriminatory basis, either within the petroleum industry or to nonpetroleum companies. Of the 23 companies responding, 20 of which have R&D departments, 16 reported at least some licensing revenues. The revenues from licensing appear in summary form in Table 3-32. Although 16 companies have some licensing revenues, only 11 disclosed the amounts of revenues generated by licensing. The total amount of licensing revenues was unexpectedly large—34-36 percent of core R&D expenditures of those companies reporting—and would

Table 3-32.   Licensing Revenues (11 companies) (millions of dollars)

Year	Total Licensing Revenues[a]	R&D$ Expenditures	Total Licensing Revenues/R&D
1974	108.6	$319.0	34%
1975	125.1	343.2	36

[a]Includes some petrochemical licensing revenues.
Source: Survey of 23 major oil companies.

appear to be in itself an incentive to efficient development of commercially viable projects. Of the remaining 7 companies surveyed, 4 have R&D departments and have no revenues from licensing, and 3 have no R&D function at all.

A profitability study was performed on the 23 responding companies using the ratio of return on equity as a quick measure. The results were that in 1975 the 3 companies that have no R&D averaged 14.4 percent return on equity, in comparison with the 23-company industry average of 13.3 percent. These 3 companies were relatively small in size. This at least gives some indication that smaller companies are able to remain competitive and profitable through licensing of the most up-to-date technology from firms within the industry. Thus, the licensing of technology not only gives the larger firms additional incentive to pursue research and development but, more importantly, lowers barriers to entry and survival for the smaller firms who might not otherwise be financially able to support a large R&D effort.

In summary, the leading petroleum companies spend large amounts of money on R&D and appear to spend somewhat more than in proportion to their size. The data on patents, commercial processes, and licensing fees, also supports a conclusion that R&D output increases with size. Companies develop commercially viable processes rather than sitting on attractive patents. Furthermore, all evidence seems to support the finding that each company or industry involved in developing new energy sources tends to focus attention in the area that is most compatible with the way the company presently does business. Accordingly, most oil companies have not focused their efforts on coal gasification, but rather on coal liquification technology, seeking to convert their coal reserves into products that can be distributed through their present channels.

Technology: Transfer and Synergy

We conclude, then, that the responding companies develop, commercialize, and license, technology. But it is also pertinent to inquire whether the possibility that technology developed in one energy area can be advantageously applied to others. The answer to this question would clearly seem to be yes. In the course of our interviews R&D executives identified numerous areas in which oil companies have provided technical expertise to the coal industry and to the mining of oil shale and or uranium. A large number of cases of specific technology transfers and synergistic effects among R&D groups will be discussed in detail later in this section.

Although most of the technology that has been transferred from one energy source to another has generally gone from the petroleum exploration, production, and refining, to coal, uranium, or synthetic fuel development, technology transfer has also gone in the opposite direction; for example, strip mining technology used in coal operations is being adapted for use in uranium and oil shale recovery.

To put this issue even more clearly in perspective, it is useful to note that prior to the petroleum companies becoming involved in either the operation of coal companies or the acquisition of reserves, only one coal company, Consolidation Coal, had any in-house R&D functions. Consolidation has stated that even at that its R&D was entirely process-oriented; the research was directed more at ways of getting the coal out of the ground than in modifying or refining coal for different uses.

Traditionally, independent coal companies have carried out their R&D through the research facilities of the Bituminous Coal Operators Association and the National Coal Association, the funds being provided by association members (prorated on a cents-per-ton basis). The executives interviewed who were members of these associations admitted to the inadequacy of both the size of their R&D budgets and the type of R&D done by these associations.[39] They attribute the lack of R&D success to lack of experience both in obtaining R&D matching funds from government and of their scientists in doing wider, broader-based research. The earlier section of this book discussed the coal industry's attitude toward price competition from petroleum-company-owned counterparts as being healthy for the industry. The independent coal operators also stated that any technology developed by petroleum companies in the area of coal mining is openly licensed, and that they had no indications that the petroleum industry is attempting to restrict the technology they developed to gain a competitive advantage over its independent competitors. As a matter of fact, some coal company representatives were convinced that, from a technological standpoint, it would be a detriment to the coal industry if the oil companies were kept out of the business.

In regard to multi-energy resource technology, the questionnaire responses of the 23 oil companies were classified into three major categories: (1) upgrading of liquid products from synthetic fuel operations; (2) improvements in operating techniques and equipment; and (3) pollution-control techniques. Within each area the following specific technologies or processes were most often identified as being applicable both in the petroleum field and in one or more other energy resource recovery areas.

1. Upgrading of Liquid Products From Synthetic Fuel Operations:

- Hydrocracking
- Desulphurization
- Denitrogenation
- Demetallation
- Coking
- Hydrorefining
- Removal of arsenic

2. Improvements in Operating Techniques and Equipment:

- Advanced computer analysis techniques for evaluating rock-cutter interaction.
- Improved methods for core sampling and analysis.
- Computer programs for determining hydrocarbon and mineral content.
- Process instrumentation.
- "In-situ" combustion techniques (previously used for petroleum adaptable to tar sands).
- Improved seismic correlation techniques.
- New soil stabilization methods for plant and pipeline foundations.
- Pipeline technology (has great potential for reducing transportation costs of tar sands and coal).
- Research done in corrosion (especially applicable to geothermal corrosion problems).
- Fluid-flow research (much application in solution mining of minerals).
- Aerial Radioactivity Surveying (ARAS) (developed for oil prospecting, has been applied to uranium prospecting).
- Seismographic technology (adapted to systems for locating trapped mineral and flooded mine tunnels).

3. Pollution Control:

- Waste-water treatment knowledge gained from experience in refining is especially useful in treating heavy fuels recovered from tar sands and geothermal deposits.

- Stack-gas cleaning developed for either petrochemical or petroleum uses are now either adaptable to commercial plants in oil shale, tar sands, and so on, or are being developed as a product in second-generation scrubbers for use by utilities.
- Oil-spill recovery experience has been extremely valuable in dealing with environmental complaints over handling of tar sands or geothermal overflows.

Several of the 23 oil companies surveyed reported that they were involved in nearly all of the foregoing technologies and alternative energy sources. Individual companies reported numerous additional examples of other technology transfers they have explored alone. Appendix C shows in detail a listing of the areas of technological synergy for one of the more active multi-resource energy companies, Continental Oil.

R&D Trends

Senator Kennedy, in the course of the hearings on horizontal divestiture, has indicated the importance of looking at the future intent as well as the present conduct of oil companies. While it is impossible to predict accurately which resources will actually end up being developed, an analysis of the areas and scope of research currently conducted by the 23 survey companies will indicate the direction in which various firms are heading, the intensity of their involvement in different resources, the gaps in their present R&D efforts, and how these gaps are being filled.

As industry sales increased over the period 1971-1975, so did expenditures on research and development.[40] These expenditures will continue to rise, although the *percentage* growth of the 1971-1975 period probably will not be maintained. Before the 1973 oil embargo crisis, the bulk of all research and development funds were expended in the area of oil and gas. The crisis prompted the government to take the long-needed step of promoting the objective of energy diversification and self-sufficiency.

Due to the finiteness of oil reserves, while the petroleum companies continued to put larger sums in oil and gas R&D, they also began to step up their R&D effort in other energy sources they believed were potentially marketable (see Figure 3-2). In 1971, 91.2 percent of the industry's investment in R&D efforts was in the area of oil and gas. By 1975 this percentage had dropped to 76.2 percent. The data appear to indicate that the percentage will level off somewhere around this point. In the same five-year period, R&D investment in coal and shale took a giant leap forward, from a bare

Figure 3-2. Trend of Specific Area Expenditures as Percent of Total R & D Budget, 1971-1975

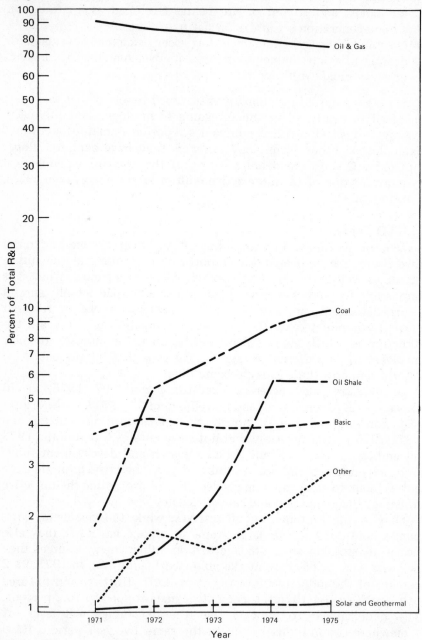

Source: Survey of 23 major oil companies.

3.3 percent of total R&D to nearly 16 percent (Table 3-33). Efforts in solar, geothermal, basic research, and other (uranium, tar sands, and so on) have increased less dramatically. However, all firms did not follow a uniform pattern. Different firms chose to go into different areas, building up varying quantities of technical know-how and available raw materials depending on their individual estimates of what the future held.

Data presented earlier in Table 3-27 showed that the largest eight reporting companies accounted for 80 percent of all R&D reported for the years 1971-1975. It is clear that these firms have spread their research efforts in varying patterns over the important energy areas, with only three of the eight firms having placed in the top third (of all firms surveyed) of more than one area (excluding oil and gas). Each of the other five has devoted its major effort to individual areas. Our survey data indicate that these trends will continue in the future. The 1976-1980 projection presents a pattern that is fairly consistent with that of 1971-1975. R&D investment in all forms of energy rise and level out at slightly higher levels (Figure 3-3). A major change apparently will take place in the area of oil shale R&D. It drops from a 1975 high of 5.7 percent back to its 1971 level of 1.4 percent. In reality this may not be the case. It may simply reflect the fact that two of the larger (though not largest) investors in shale did not furnish their projections in this area.

An examination of the industry on a firm-by-firm basis points to the high level of variation that exists. The situation should lead to the greatest potential for self-sufficiency by virtue of the fact that all bases are being covered by technologically sophisticated R&D establishments. Additionally, the diverse patterns of R&D that the larger companies are emphasizing would appear to further reduce the potential for tacit collusion.

Development Examples

The different patterns of investment in energy are a function of technical know-how, resource availability, and projections of what the future holds. The determining considerations, however, for large as well as small firms, is actual or prospective return on investment. Obviously the former variables affect the latter. Ability to transfer technology may lower development costs, thereby leading to a potentially higher return on investment. The creation of new technologies may make it possible to use resources and reserves formerly unused, and hence increase revenues.

The alternative approaches toward investment in various energy sources are brought out in the following cases. While these cases

Figure 3-3.   Projected Trend of Specific Area Expenditures as Percent of Total R & D Budget, 1975-1980

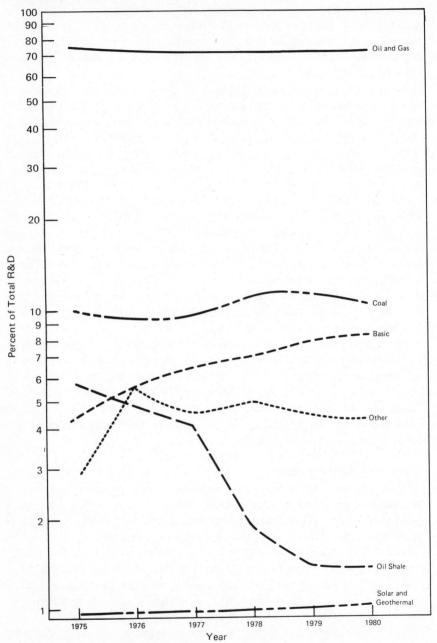

Source: Survey of 23 major oil companies.

point to the divergent patterns within the industry, they also show that smaller firms consider it necessary to have holdings in alternative energies in order to assure their survival.

Oil Shale. Two of the largest investors in oil shale research and development, Union and Occidental, are among the smaller of the top 25 oil companies. As is clear here, and becomes even more obvious as one examines the many firms in the industry, involvement in a less popular energy alternative today is perceived as one method of securing a niche for the future in the energy business. Union has been a pioneer in oil shale development since 1921 when it acquired land in Colorado. Its experience in handling "junky" California crude oil provided insights into how to extract oil from equally "junky" shale.

Occidental may be the only firm to finance oil shale development entirely with its own funds. The company invested large sums of money to create an in-situ process. The March 1976 issue of *Synthetic Fuels* quotes Executive V.P. Donald Baeder, as saying about shale:

> We have spent 5 years and over $30 million in this major pioneering endeavor, and we have done it alone. Provided that our preliminary economics continue to be substantial, we are prepared to spend more to prove and improve our technology. Recent Congressional action denying government guaranteed loans to pioneers of synthetic fuels technology has in no way deterred us from going forward with our program. . . . If the [5,000 BPD operation] is successful, we would bring our shale oil operations to commercial proportions as soon as possible. . . .

Coal: Research and development in the coal industry was virtually nonexistent prior to the oil companies' participation in ownership and development of coal resources. As one of America's major resources, it is an almost perfect example of one being developed in different forms depending on the strengths of the firms and the needs of the market. Because of the oil industry involvement, virtually all coal may eventually become usable, irrespective of its quality or location.

Conoco, with its large holdings of East Coast high-sulphur coal, considers the scrubber to be the key to the future of coal-related technology. Since the early 1970s Conoco has spent considerable amounts to develop a second-generation scrubber to render its high-sulphur coal usable. Exxon, on the other hand, like many major oil companies, has large holdings of low-sulphur western coal. It is faced with a different problem—high transportation costs. To resolve this problem they developed and patented a flexible coal liquefaction process that they believe is both operable and reliable. Exxon is attempting to commercialize this process in concert with ERDA. The resulting technology will be available to all interested parties.

Tar Sands: The Canadian government has control over most North American tar sands reserves. Its development and export to the United States is in large measure dependent on the current position of the Canadian government. Texaco is investigating the potential of Canadian tar sands as a future source of crude oil with an in-situ pilot project. Similarly, Sun Oil Company has made large investments in this area, and now has a commercial plant in operation. Other companies are also known to be involved.

Geothermal: Union has committed a major investment to the development of geothermal energy. This is an area of high technological synergy. For example, assurances of long-term supply (15-20 years) are essential before utility companies will become involved. Reservoir yield prediction techniques borrowed from those developed for oil and gas exploration enable long-term assurances to be given. On the other hand, methods developed for drilling geothermal wells (hard-rock drilling) are increasingly being used in drilling for oil in deep deposits. The heat-balance mathematics so crucial in geothermal energy development is an area of expertise of oil company engineers.

Geothermal also provides an excellent example of the breadth of corporate involvement in alternative energy sources. With all the problems inherent in its development, there were still 551 bidders for leases in eleven states for the period ending January 31, 1974. These included oil companies of all sizes, geothermal companies, a state university, a rural electric cooperative, and a number of individuals. Many had filed in more than one state. This is obviously not seen as a closed market dominated by a few large entities, but as an area open for development by anyone willing and able to undertake the risks involved.

Uranium: Kerr-McGee, a relatively small oil company, is the largest developer of uranium reserves. In 1950 Kerr-McGee ranked fifth out of eleven uranium mining firms and produced 250 tons, 9.4 percent of total production. By 1960, with the increased interest in the possibility of nuclear energy, its involvement grew to where it became number one in a field of twenty-one, with 3,329 tons and 18.8 percent of total production. With the future of nuclear energy uncertain, the producers of uranium dropped to thirteen by 1975, and while Kerr-McGee was still number one, producing 15.8 percent of total production, its output was down to 1,800 tons.

CONCLUSION

Several questions must be answered before a change in the structure of the energy industry should be considered. What firms or persons currently have the technical knowledge and sophistication to fill the gap if the oil companies are divested of their holdings? If it is possible to maintain the current organizational structure within these R&D shops, or to create new ones, how will they be funded? How could divestiture affect the American public in terms of energy costs and the timing of the availability of various energy sources?

Conclusions about these questions to be drawn from the foregoing analysis are neither numerous nor complex. They are simply this: petroleum companies spend large amounts of money on research and development both in absolute dollar terms and as a percentage of total energy R&D expenditures of the private sector of the economy. Recently the R&D effort of oil companies has shifted from an exclusive concern with oil and gas to the development of alternative energy sources. There is no evidence that these expenditures on nonpetroleum energy are for the purpose of sitting on a particular new technology. On the contrary, they have significantly promoted the utilization of non-oil technology far above what it otherwise would have been.

The petroleum companies have been acting far from monolithically in the R&D area; they have spent their money on significantly different resources and technologies. All of the above factors indicate that the petroleum companies' involvement in alternative energy sources from a technological standpoint is to be desired. Given the size of the R&D establishments found in the petroleum industry, it is highly doubtful that other firms in the private sector would take them over, or create new ones of comparable size to take their place. Additional government funding could, of course, fill the void by providing the necessary dollars and personnel; however, the historical record has shown government agencies to be ineffective in translating invention into development and commercialization.

The pattern of R&D expenditures by major oil companies is entirely consistent with the aims of national policy on energy research. If we judge national R&D priorities from federal expenditure of funds, energy research ranks near the top. In 1976 the energy agency's R&D budget increased to $2.8 billion, a 35 percent jump over that appropriated in 1975, ranking it third among all federal agency R&D spending (behind only the Department of Defense and NASA). In 1977 an additional 17 percent increase is expected in R&D funds spent by ERDA. Most of this increase in R&D is directed toward the development of non-oil energy sources, the same area where petroleum companies are increasing their R&D budgets.

NOTES

1. In order for firms to be considered competitive and in the same market they must supply close-substitute outputs to a common group of buyers. Cf. Joe S. Bain, *Industrial Organization* (2nd ed.; New York: Wiley, 1968), p. 124.

2. Office of Science and Technology, *Patterns of Energy Consumption in the U.S.* (Washington: U.S. Government Printing Office, 1972), p. 145.

3. Federal Trade Commission (FTC), *Concentration Levels and Trends in the Energy Sector of the U.S. Economy*, 1974, p. 13.

4. Ibid., p. 6.

5. Bureau of Mines data.

6. Federal Energy Administration, *National Energy Outlook* (FEA-N-75/713), February 1976, p. 21.

7. Cameron Engineers, *Synthetic Fuels: Quarterly Report*, March 1976.

8. It should be noted that price parallelism has been held to be evidence of oil company/coal company collusion, while it should be the expected result of free-market forces in any case where products are substitutable.

9. FTC, *Concentration Levels and Trends in the Energy Sector of the U.S. Economy*, p. 9.

10. David Schwartzman, "The Cross-Elasticity of Demand and Industry Boundaries: Coal, Oil, Gas, and Uranium," *Antitrust Bulletin* 17 (Fall 1973): p. 507.

11. The FPC data have significant advantages over those available from other sources (such as the Bureau of Labor Statistics), for they are reported on a "delivered basis" and therefore represent a true cost to the utility of the fuel at the power generating plant.

12. President's Council on Wage and Price Stability, *A Study of Coal Prices*, March 1976.

13. For a more detailed discussion of the technological and environmental constraints, see FEA, *National Energy Outlook*, p. 169.

14. T. Duchesneau, *Competition in the U.S. Energy Industry* (Cambridge: Ballinger Publishing Co., 1975), p. 22.

15. Federal Power Commission, *The Potential for Conversion of Oil-Fired and Gas-Fired Electric Generating Units to the Use of Coal*, Staff Report, 1973, p. 1.

16. It is emphasized that the line of reasoning here proceeds for the sake of argument only. As developed at length in Chapter 2, the level of concentration in the energy industry and its constituent subsectors is much too low to assume that oil companies will in fact act as a tight-knit oligopoly.

17. As part of this study interviews were held with a number of key executives in various sectors of the energy industry.

18. Federal Energy Administration, *National Energy Outlook*, p. 200.

19. Ibid.

20. FTC, *Concentration Levels and Trends in the Energy Sector of the U.S. Economy*, pp. 119-20. The charges are for an average haul of 231 miles.

21. Richard L. Gordon, *U.S. Coal and Electric Power Industry* (New York: Resources for the Future, 1975), p. 42.

22. Bankers Trust Company, "Capital Resources for Energy through the Year 1990," New York, 1976.

23. For assumptions underlying this breakdown, see ibid.

24. *Basic Estimated Capital Investment and Operating Costs for Underground Bituminous Coal Mines*, Bureau of Mines Information Circular 8689, (Washington, 1975), Table 2.

25. A provocative analysis of our economic ills is contained in Arthur Jones, *The Decline of Capital* (New York: Crowell, 1976).

26. Benjamin J. Friedman, "Financing the Next Five Years of Fixed Investment," *Sloan Management Review*, Spring 1975.

27. These scenarios were developed in a recent report to the Environmental Protection Agency, "Economic and Financial Impacts of Federal Air and Water Pollution Controls on the Electric Utility Industry," (EPA-203/3-76-013), May 1976.

28. FEA, *National Energy Outlook*, p. 293.

29. Ibid., pp. 322, 323.

30. Bankers Trust Company, "Capital Resources for Energy through the Year 1990," p. 23.

31. That electric utilities could be expected to be a prime source of investment capital for the coal industry is indicated by the increase in utility-captive coal mine production as a percentage of total U.S. production from 2.3 percent in 1971 to 7 percent in 1975. Given the utilities' severely constrained financial condition, this increase would no doubt have been much greater had they had free access to funds. *Keystone Coal Annual*, 1971; and *Keystone News Bulletins*, 1975.

32. W.T. Hogan, "New Capacity for Steelmaking by 1980: How Much and What Products?" Steel Service Center Institute, 1975.

33. *Business' Plans for New Plant and Equipment* (New York: McGraw-Hill, 1971-1975).

34. *Oil Daily*, November 14, 1976.

35. Jerome E. Hass et al., *Financing the Energy Industry* (Cambridge: Ballinger Publishing Co., 1974), p. 2.

36. The $6.5 billion annual investment requirement is derived from the data in Table 3-17 as follows: the 10-year "best" estimates fall in the range $40-90 billion. The midpoint estimate of $65 billion equals an annual average of $6.5 billion.

37. "Market Structure and the Employment of Scientists and Engineers," *American Economic Review* (June 1967), pp. 529, 530.

38. NSF, *Research and Development in Industry* (#75-315), 1973, p. 53.

39. BCOA members typically contribute 1¢ per ton mined as dues, about one-third of which goes into research. This translates into $1-2 million in R&D funds which, together with about the same amount of government funds, serves as the association's total R&D budget.

40. The relationship between sales and R&D expenditures is illustrated in Table 3-27.

Table 3-33. Research Outlays by Major Oil Companies by Type of Energy, 1971-1980[1]

	1971	1972	1973	1974	1975	1976	1977	1978	1979	1980
Total R&D Expenditures (000)	286,465	326,651	361,702	458,029	510,306	456,369[2]	443,000[2]	483,127[2]	513,127[2]	538,068[2]
Total Oil & Gas (000)	261,396	282,210	306,706	362,993	388,842	337,844	330,225	356,975	379,300	398,086
% of Total R&D	91.2	86.4	84.8	79.3	76.2	74.0	74.5	73.9	73.9	74.0
Total Shale (000)	3,971	5,046	8,302	25,432	28,893	22,549	18,240	8,190	6,990	7,290
% of Total R&D	1.4	1.5	2.3	5.6	5.7	4.9	4.1	1.7	1.4	1.4
Total Coal (000)	5,526	18,295	24,814	39,210	51,018	42,428	42,612	56,126	59,811	56,497
% of Total R&D	1.9	5.6	6.9	8.6	10.0	9.3	9.6	11.6	11.6	10.5
Total Solar (000)	1,024	1,024	1,053	2,261	4,525	1,380	2,370	3,370	4,570	5,770
% of Total R&D	.4	.3	.3	.5	.9	.3	.5	.7	.9	1.1
Total Geothermal (000)	173	188	208	363	891	1,180	1,220	1,270	1,370	1,420
% of Total R&D	.06	.05	.06	.07	.2	.3	.3	.3	.3	.3
Total Other (000)	3,161	5,924	5,293	9,574	14,551	25,348	19,933	23,796	22,004	23,505
% of Total R&D	1.1	1.8	1.5	2.1	2.9	5.6	4.5	4.9	4.3	4.4
Total Basic (000)	11,214	13,964	14,478	18,196	21,586	25,644	28,400	33,400	39,500	43,500
% of Total R&D	3.9	4.3	4.0	4.0	4.2	5.6	6.4	6.9	7.7	8.1

1. Source: Survey of 23 petroleum companies.
2. Excluding two companies who did not furnish projected data.

Chapter Four

The Pro-Competitive Structural Aspects of Horizontal Diversification

Much of this study has been concerned with the issue of whether horizontal diversification by petroleum companies into other sectors of the energy industry might lead to a reduction of competition and efficiency in those sectors. The analysis of the structure of the energy industry strongly supports the conclusion that it would not. In addition, the empirical evidence shows that, for both economic and technological reasons, petroleum firms are the most likely and efficient entrants into other sectors of the energy industry, and hence that preclusion of horizontal diversification by petroleum firms can be expected to retard technological progress and the rate of investment in the energy industry. The implications of such preclusion for the U.S. economy as a whole are obvious.

Moreover, horizontal diversification by petroleum firms is not only technologically and economically beneficial, but strategically procompetitive, as well. Recent developments in the economic theory of industrial organization suggest that not only will horizontal diversification by petroleum companies be unlikely to lead to a reduction in competition in the energy industry, but that the "asymmetry" among firms to which such diversification leads may well increase significantly the degree of competition in the industry and thus make even more remote the possibility of tacit collusion among energy suppliers.

ASYMMETRY DEFINED

The proposition that asymmetry is an important determinant of workable competition is rather complex and sophisticated and, to date, has generated discussion limited almost entirely to academic circles. Neither of these facts, however, argues against consideration of examining its implications for horizontal divestiture; the energy industry is sufficiently important to the U.S. economy to require that any legislation proposing to dramatically alter its structure and future growth be based upon a sophisticated rather than a simplistic understanding of the economics of industrial organization.

One of the first major discussions of asymmetry as a determinant of competition in an industry appeared in Michael Hunt's 1972 industry study of the major home appliance industry.[1] Since World War II the structure of that industry, whose products include refrigerators, clothes washers and dryers, kitchen ranges, dishwashers, sink disposal units, and trash compactors, had changed dramatically; concentration of sales among a small group of manufacturers had occurred, product differentiation had greatly increased, and there had been a considerable heightening of the barriers-to-entry into the industry. Yet competition in terms of performance of the industry was quite evident.

A central conclusion of Hunt's examination of competition in the industry was that the asymmetry among the various firms' strategies, product lines, and objectives was responsible for the industry's highly satisfactory competitive performance. Asymmetry, even in the face of a rising trend in concentration, had caused the firms' conduct to be highly competitive, resulting in a highly satisfactory outcome from a public policy viewpoint. The focus on asymmetry initiated by Hunt continues to receive the attention of students of industrial organization.[2]

The asymmetry argument and its implications for public policy can be defined as follows: (1) Asymmetry means dissimilarity between competing firms' assets, organizational structures, product lines, business strategies, and objectives. (2) As the degree of asymmetry between competitors increases, the likelihood that they can advantageously pursue an identical joint profit-maximizing form of behavior decreases. Hence, asymmetry reduces the incentive for, and possibility of, tacit or overt collusion among competitors. One can best appreciate the logic of this proposition by examining its obverse side; namely, the more symmetric or similar to each other competitors are (with respect to their asset bases, goals, strategies, products, and so on) the more likely could there exist some common form of joint profit-maximizing behavior. Therefore, in these circumstances, collusive or cooperative behavior on the part of these competitors is a possibility, provided the prerequisite structural conditions for parallel action exist. A moment's reflection on the above proposition should confirm its inherent logic, and hence explain why asymmetry among member firms of an industry is an important deterrent to tacit collusion.

ASYMMETRY IN THE PETROLEUM INDUSTRY

In addition to the low level of concentration in the oil industry, and in the energy industry generally, there currently exists a considerable degree of asymmetry among the major petroleum companies. The extent of this asymmetry will be developed presently. More important to the present argument, however, is the understanding that regardless of what level of asymmetry one currently perceives as existing between the major petroleum companies, horizontal diversification by them into different alternate energy fields can only lead to an even greater degree of asymmetry among their asset bases, products, organizational structures, strategies, and objectives, and therefore make them more likely to compete with each other. In other words, even if we were disposed to argue that in the face of the relatively low level of concentration in the industry the eight, the dozen, or the eighteen "pure" petroleum companies—that is, those holding nearly all of their reserves in the form of oil and gas—might pursue a common course of action, it is highly unlikely that the same number of firms would perceive as profitable such a course of action should they attain a considerable degree of diversity among themselves through horizontal diversification. In time, the varying percentages of their assets relating to oil, gas, coal, uranium, oil shale, geothermal deposits, and the like would greatly reduce the possibility of there existing a common course of action equally suited to them all.

It would seem to follow from this that those who maintain that the present level of concentration in the oil industry is conducive to tacit collusion among the major petroleum companies should welcome the prospects of horizontal diversification since, once asymmetry is taken into consideration, such diversification can be expected to make such collusion more difficult. That they have opposed rather than welcomed this diversification is largely attributable to their having overlooked the current level of asymmetry among petroleum companies.

Simplistic interpretations of current industry conduct are frequently based on the implicit assumption that there exists a high level of similarity among the major firms' assets, resources, operations, and goals. This assumption is not always consistent with the facts. For example, although all of the major eight petroleum companies are vertically integrated, their domestic self-sufficiency ratios in 1969 ranged all the way from 42.2 percent (for Mobil) to 87.6 percent (for Gulf). Even if one looks at petroleum companies of similar size there is a considerable degree of dissimilarity among their sources of revenue; a comparison of two petroleum companies of similar size illustrates this point. In terms of revenues the Amerada Hess Corporation and the Cities Service Company are nearly identical in size; in 1975 Amerada Hess had revenues of $3.214 billion and Cities Service had sales of $3.2 billion.[3] An analysis of their North American operations in that year, however, indicates the underlying dissimilarity of the two companies (see Table 4-1). Although Amerada Hess and Cities Service had almost identical crude oil production, their natural gas production and refining operations were dramatically different.

A further comparison would reveal that Cities Service was heavily involved in plastics, industrial chemicals, and metals, while the Amerada Hess organization had no interests in any of these products. A comparison between either of these two petroleum companies and the similarly sized Getty Oil Company (1975 sales of $3.175 billion) would also reveal considerable differences in their operations.

This dissimilarity exists at all levels of size in the industry, as comparisons of other matched pairs confirm. A pair of larger petroleum companies, Phillips and Union Oil, are approximately the

Table 4-1. Comparison of Amerada Hess with Cities Service, Selected North American Operations, 1975

Amerada Hess		*Cities Service*	
Production of Crude Oil and Liquids, barrels per day, U.S. and Canada	113,785	Production of Crude Oil, net barrels daily, North America	117,200
Production of Natural Gas, million cubic feet per day, U.S. and Canada	434,057	Production of Natural Gas, million cubic feet per day, North America	1,007,400
Marketing and Refining— barrels per day:		Marketing and Refining— barrels per day:	
Refined products sold	523,000	Petroleum products sold	359,000
Refinery runs	519,000	Refinery runs	249,500

Source: Corporate annual reports.

same size in terms of total revenues; in 1975 Union Oil had sales of $5.5 billion and Phillips had sales of $5.2 billion. Examination of their respective operations, however, reveals a considerable degree of dissimilarity between the two corporations despite their similar size. Table 4-2 presents a selection of operating statistics for the two companies.[4]

A further comparison of either Union Oil or Phillips with similarly sized Occidental ($5.35 billion sales in 1975) would also reveal significant differences: unlike Union Oil or Phillips, Occidental derives a considerable amount of revenue from the sale of coal ($658.8 million in 1975) and a much greater proportion of its total revenue from its chemical operations, $1.585 billion in 1975 versus $981.8 million and $415.9 million, respectively, for Phillips and Union Oil.

A comparison of the operations of two of the giants of the industry, Exxon and Texaco, reveals comparable degrees of dissimilarity. These two companies are considerably different in size; Exxon had 1975 revenues of $48.8 billion, while Texaco had revenues of $25.1 billion.[5] As Table 4-3 indicates, however, despite being approximately half the size of Exxon in terms of sales, Texaco had a larger gross production of crude oil and natural gas liquids and has nearly as much crude oil and natural gas reserves as Exxon. In other words, even the two largest petroleum companies are operationally quite dissimilar.[a]

CONCLUSIONS

It would seem reasonable to conclude that it would be more difficult for an energy company that held 60 percent of its resources in the form of oil and gas, 20 percent in oil shale deposits, and 20 percent in coal to come to some collusive arrangement with another energy

Table 4-2. Selected Operating Statistics, 1975

	Phillips Petroleum	Union Oil
Net Daily Production of Crude Oil (barrels):	246,000	313,200
Daily Production of Natural Gas Liquids (barrels):	140,000	34,000
Daily Natural Gas Production (thousand cubic feet):	1,665,000	1,442,200
Petroleum Products Sold (barrels daily):	658,000	449,000

Source: Corporate annual reports.

[a]Further factual evidence of the dissimilarity among petroleum companies appears in the tables in Appendix B.

Table 4-3. Selected Statistics, 1975

	Texaco	Exxon
Gross Crude Oil and Natural Gas Liquids Production (thousands of barrels daily)	3,770	3,684
Total Proved Reserves of Crude Oil and Natural Gas Liquids (millions of barrels)	20,695	23,318
Refinery Runs of Crude Oil, Natural Gas Liquids and Distillates (thousands of barrels daily)	2,772	4,331[a]
Petroleum Product Sales (thousands of barrels daily)	3,241	4,990
Natural Gas Sales (millions of cubic feet daily)	4,035	9,658

[a]Exxon figure represents refinery crude oil runs only.

Source: Corporate annual reports and statistical supplements.

company holding 50 percent of its resources in oil and gas, 40 percent in uranium, and 10 percent in geothermal, than if both companies produced only oil and gas. This difficulty is greatly magnified when both such companies are in competition with a host of other energy companies having varying degrees of asymmetry. Hence, it is logical to conclude that a legislative environment that fosters the development of the greatest possible variety of resource mixes in energy producers is far more conducive to the maintenance of workable competition in the energy industry than one that forces a straitjacket of conformity upon its member firms.

The prevailing degree of asymmetry in the energy industry will be increased if oil companies are allowed to continue their diverse paths of horizontal diversification. The diversity of petroleum companies' horizontal diversification strategies has been dealt with earlier in this study. Some companies have acquired or developed coal resources while shunning oil shale and geothermal deposits; others have developed geothermal and oil shale deposits while ignoring uranium and coal resources; still others have not diversified horizontally to any significant degree at all. The pattern, effected through horizontal diversification, however, is one of increasing asymmetry among the major petroleum companies. Legislation that would preclude this important means for increased asymmetry, and hence increased competition, could well achieve results diametrically opposed to its stated objectives.

There is an additional and more familiar procompetitive aspect of horizontal diversification. Freedom of entry into an industry is universally held by economists of all persuasions to be an extremely important determinant of competition. Since the Horizontal Divestiture Bill (S.489) would eliminate petroleum companies as entrants, either potential or actual, into other sectors of the energy industry, it would not only constitute a serious departure from normal antitrust policy but, in effect, be in direct opposition to the preservation of the "highest degree of freedom-of-entry possible," which has, to date, been the objective of the antitrust laws. The Horizontal Divestiture Bill is in conflict with this long-standing antitrust objective. When one further considers the fact that petroleum companies—due to their expertise in managing capital-intensive, long-lead-time, high-technology, natural resource projects—are logical candidates for entry into other sectors of the energy industry, the anticompetitive character of the Horizontal Divestiture Bill becomes even more apparent.[b] To preclude the entry of companies whose capabilities and policies make them remote candidates for entry into an industry might have few if any anticompetitive consequences, but to preclude the entry of the most likely, capable, and eager group of entrants—the petroleum companies—is clearly in conflict with a basic public policy that preserves "potential" entrants on the grounds that they are likely eventually to enter. Not only are the effective barriers-to-entry into alternate energy sectors of the industry heightened through government action, but an important stimulus to competitive behavior in those alternate energy sectors—the threat of entry by new competitors—is significantly reduced. Horizontal divestiture will not only reduce the levels of asymmetry among petroleum companies, it will also preclude the development, or reduce the existence, of asymmetry among coal companies, uranium producers, shale oil producers, and other energy companies. Hence, the Horizontal Divestiture Bill will not only have adverse effects on future competitors in the petroleum industry, but in the nonpetroleum sectors of the energy industry as well.

NOTES

1. Michael Hunt, "Competition in the Major Home Appliance Industry," unpublished doctoral thesis, Harvard University, 1972.

2. Michael E. Porter, *Interbrand Choice, Strategy, and Bilateral Market Power* (Cambridge: Harvard University Press, 1976).

3. *1975 Annual Report*, Amerada Hess Corporation and Cities Service Company.

4. *1975 Annual Report*, Union Oil Company and Phillips Petroleum Company.

5. *1975 Annual Report*, and statistical supplements, Texaco and Exxon, Inc.

[b]This line of argument pertains especially to the entry by petroleum companies into nonpetroleum energy industries through internal expansion. In certain circumstances it could pertain to entry by merger, such as an oil company's acquisition of a "toe-hold" non-oil company for purposes of greatly expanding its operations.

Chapter Five

Conclusions

The main argument put forward in support of horizontal divestiture is that should petroleum companies acquire significant alternate energy resources, they will not actively pursue the development of these resources. Rather, they will restrict their output in order to minimize interfuel competition and thereby maintain the highest possible prices for their petroleum and gas products in order to protect the value of their petroleum and gas reserves. This has been labeled the "withholding-of-production theory" and it has been frequently cited in the speeches, writings, and testimony of proponents of horizontal divestiture legislation.[a]

The withholding-of-production theory is in sharp conflict with the logic of the behavioral advantages of multi-energy resource firms described in the previous chapter of this study. Specifically, our investigation supports the following conclusions, none of which provides support to the withholding-production theory.

THERE IS NO NEED FOR STRUCTURAL REMEDIES

The Level of Concentration is Low. No single petroleum company controls a large enough share of the petroleum or energy industry, regardless of the industry definition used, to give that

---

[a]For example, see the remarks and questions of Senator Abourezk at the Hearings before the Subcommittee on Antitrust and Monopoly of the Committee on the Judiciary, United States Senate, 94th Congress, on S. 489, the Interfuel Competition Act of 1975, July 14, 1975, pp. 191-195.

company the power to significantly affect the prices of the various energy products, including oil, gas, coal, and uranium. No company has a sufficient market share to make it either possible or worthwhile for it to withhold its output in one sector of the energy industry in an attempt to increase the prices of its products in any other sector of the industry. Petroleum companies, even the largest ones, are price-takers, and no firm has a sufficient share of total production to manipulate the relative prices of the various forms of energy. Given the market concentration statistics, the price-manipulating powers implied in the withholding-of-production argument simply do not exist.

Tacit Collusion is Improbable.   Since the level of concentration in the energy industry (or petroleum industry) is well below the cut-off point where tacit collusion becomes a reasonable possibility, it cannot be maintained that, through tacit collusion or oligopolistic coordination, a *group* of petroleum firms could exert the stranglehold on production that the withholding-of-production argument implies. Furthermore, the significant degree of asymmetry among petroleum companies would militate against the development of tacit collusion even if unforeseeably higher levels of concentration in the energy industry should materialize.

Existing Antitrust Laws can Prevent Anticompetitive Behavior. Finally, the various antitrust laws may be applied to prevent anticompetitive behavior on the part of members of the petroleum industry. In view of its relatively low concentration, any withholding-of-production type of conduct on the part of petroleum companies would require either overt or covert agreements that generate direct evidence of conspiracy. Forestalling and engrossing by single entities and by consortia are ancient and familiar monopoly practices that antitrust agencies should have little difficulty in detecting and prosecuting. But since in this case the offense is not related to structure, a structural remedy is inappropriate. Moreover, the fact that there is a relatively low level of interfuel substitutability makes the rationale for a policy of cross-market synchronization implied by the withholding-of-production argument even less tenable.

WITHHOLDING-OF-PRODUCTION WOULD BE IRRATIONAL

In addition to, and apart from, the structural considerations outlined above, the withholding-of-production argument is untenable because it would be illogical for horizontally diversified petroleum companies to restrict the output of expanding sectors of the energy industry in order to obtain at best uncertain marginal gains for their oil and gas products. If the entire energy industry were highly concentrated in the hands of a few large diversified companies, they collectively might conceivably forego sales in a minor stable market in order to maintain sales in their major markets; however, it would not be reasonable for a diversified company or group of companies to restrict output in major and expanding markets in order to effect a minor and most uncertain gain in their other markets.

Because it is the alternate energy sectors of the energy industry that will have the highest growth rates in the future, it would be illogical for diversified petroleum companies to withhold their production of these forms of energy. In fact, the economic motivation for petroleum companies' acquisition of such alternate energy resources as coal, uranium, oil shale, geothermal deposits, and so on is the belief on the part of these companies' top management that, in order for their companies to continue to grow, they must actively engage in the development and expansion of these increasingly important sources of energy. As Figure 5-1 indicates, a major domestic source of the energy problem in the U.S. is the complete mismatch between the prevailing energy consumption pattern and the nation's energy reserves pattern.

Figure 5-1. Energy Resource Reserves and Consumption Pattern

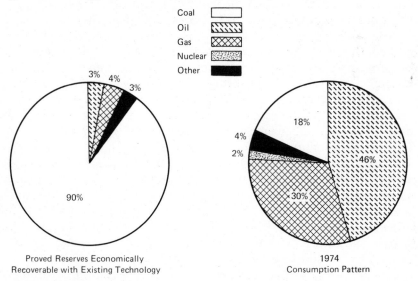

Source: FEA, *1976 National Energy Outlook*, February 1976, p. xxii.

If the current energy problem is to be alleviated, this imbalance will have to be rectified. The nation cannot continue to depend upon its least abundant major energy resources (oil and gas) to provide most of its energy needs. In 1975 the U.S. Bureau of Mines published its projection of U.S. consumption of energy by major sources and consuming sectors up to the year 2000 (see Table 5-1). The projections indicate a significant growth in the consumption of all types of energy over the next twenty-five years, with the exception of natural gas consumption. However, by far the most rapid rates of consumption growth will be in the areas of nuclear power and coal. The suspicion that large petroleum companies seeking to become large energy companies through horizontal diversification would voluntarily withhold their production in these key growth industries is surely unfounded, especially when one cannot realistically see how they might convert such behavior into tangible gains, given the structure of the industry and the low level of interfuel substitutability.

Finally, in an economy where energy demand is exerting great pressure on supply, the withholding-of-production argument loses its essential rationale. Regardless of oligopolistic aspirations and alleged tendencies to pursue a common course of action, it simply does not make sense for diversified petroleum companies to attempt to withhold production of *any* source of energy when major shortages of all sources of energy at existing prices make possible the sale of more of all forms of energy in the long run. In these circumstances an output restriction policy is irrational, even for oligopolists, much less for members of a relatively unconcentrated industry. While one can, under certain conditions, build a rationale for the withholding of production of a product in excess supply, the same rationale does not apply when there is a shortage at present prices of that product.

In a free market, of course, shortages are eliminated through price increases; the persistence of an energy shortage can be attributed to many factors, of which the absence of free-market conditions—several energy products' prices continue to be regulated—the significant lead times of several years between the finding of new energy sources and their commercialization, and the instability of foreign energy supplies and prices are among the most important. Few competent observers of the energy situation question the existence of a shortage, and most expect it to continue well into the foreseeable future. All the forecasts of domestic energy supply/ demand trends find the greatest domestic supply shortfall in the oil sector. While the various forecasts differ on the exact magnitude of the shortfall, they agree on the main conclusion—a continued shortage of domestic oil, which will result in the continued growth of oil imports and accelerated use of such alternative sources of energy as coal, oil shale, and uranium.

Table 5-2 summarizes the results of 1985 liquid-fuel forecasts prepared by the Chase Manhattan Bank, Stanford Research Institute, National Petroleum Council, and Shell Oil Company. As can be seen from these forecasts the percentage of total demand for liquid fuels in the United States that will be met by imports ranges from 50.3 to as much as 65.5 percent. Even after allowance is made for increases in the supply of domestic coal, gas, and other energy sources, there will continue to exist an oil deficit that will have to be met through increases in imports (Figure 5-2). With a projected excess of demand over domestic supply for all forms of energy, the petroleum companies have no incentive to withhold production of any one type of energy for the purpose of maintaining the sales of another.[b] All of the preceding points toward the real reason oil companies have moved into alternative energy areas. The day is approaching when demand for nonresidual products (gasoline, home heating oil, and so on) will be great enough to permit all crude to be refined into such products. The value of these products has traditionally been much greater than that of residual fuel oil (see Table 5-3). This will force production-constrained oil companies to withdraw from fuel-oil markets such as the utility markets, gradually leaving a vacuum to be filled *unless* they fill it themselves by developing nonpetroleum energy resources. This is profit-maximization behavior, economically rational, and competitive.

[b]One should note that the charge that oil and gas companies have followed policies of withholding some of their production—specifically of gas—and thereby of contriving an energy shortage, is not a new one. However, in every instance where a thorough investigation has been conducted the charge has not been supported by the evidence. Arguments that oil and gas producers have been shutting in gas reserves have been raised and rejected in area rate proceedings by the Federal Power Commission, by the United States Court of Appeals for the District of Columbia, by the Fifth and Ninth Circuit Courts, and by the Federal Power Commission's Natural Gas Survey. (See testimony by Rogers Morton, former Secretary of the Interior, before the U.S. Senate Commerce Committee, December 4, 1974.)

Table 5-1.   U.S. Consumption of Energy Resources by Major Sources and Consuming Sectors, 1974 Preliminary and Projected to the Year 2000 (trillion Btu)

Consuming Sector	Coal	Petroleum	Natural Gas	Oil Shale	Nuclear Power	Hydropower and Geothermal	Total Gross Energy Inputs	Synthetic Liquids Distributed	Synthetic Gas Distributed	Utility Electricity Distributed	Total Net Energy Inputs
1974											
Household & Commercial	291	6,390	7,116	–	–	–	13,797	–	–	3,687	17,484
Industrial[a]	4,208	6,044	11,129	–	–	–	21,415	–	–	2,665	24,081
Transportation	2	17,608	654	–	–	34	18,274	–	–	16	18,290
Electrical generation	8,668	3,448	3,328	–	1,173	3,018	19,635	–	–	–	–
Synthetic gas	–	–	–	–	–	–	–	–	–	–	–
Synthetic liquids	–	–	–	–	–	–	–	–	–	–	–
Total	13,169	33,490	22,237	–	1,173	3,052	73,121	–	–	6,368	59,855
1980											
Household & Commercial	100	7,600	8,000	–	–	–	15,700	–	110	5,790	21,600
Industrial	4,800	7,500	10,000	–	–	–	22,300	–	–	3,600	25,900
Transportation	–	20,700	600	–	–	–	21,300	–	–	60	21,360
Electrical generation	12,250	5,100	2,000	–	4,550	3,800	27,700	–	–	–	–
Synthetic gas	–	140	–	–	–	–	140	–	–	–	–
Synthetic liquids	–	–	–	–	–	–	–	–	–	–	–
Total	17,150	41,040	20,600	–	4,500	3,800	87,140	–	110	9,450	68,860

1985

Household & Commercial	100	7,880	8,500	—	—	—	16,480	120	210	7,810	24,620
Industrial	4,930	8,370	9,500	—	—	—	22,800	130	240	5,620	28,790
Transportation	—	23,040	600	—	—	—	23,640	360	—	80	24,080
Electrical generation	15,700	6,200	1,500	—	11,840	3,850	39,090	—	—	—	—
Synthetic gas	520	140	—	—	—	—	660	—	—	—	—
Synthetic liquids	—	—	—	870	—	—	870	—	—	—	—
Total	21,250	45,630	20,100	870	11,840	3,850	103,540	610	450	13,510	77,490

2000

Household & Commercial	—	7,960	9,000	—	—	—	16,960	940	1,940	14,740	34,580
Industrial	5,910	10,370	9,000	—	—	—	25,280	1,230	2,260	14,680	43,450
Transportation	—	28,170	600	—	—	—	28,770	3,330	—	100	32,200
Electrical generation	20,700	4,700	1,000	—	46,000	6,070	78,550	—	—	—	—
Synthetic gas	6,000	—	—	—	—	—	6,000	—	—	—	—
Synthetic liquids	2,140	—	—	5,730	—	—	7,870	—	—	—	—
Total	34,750	51,200	19,600	5,730	46,000	6,070	163,430	5,500	4,200	29,520	110,230

[a]Miscellaneous and unaccounted energy assigned to this sector. For 1974 this was 219 trillion Btu of petroleum products.

Source: Cameron Engineers, *Synthetic Fuels: Quarterly Report*, March 1976, pp. 1-3.

Table 5-2. Forecasts of Domestic Liquid-Fuel Supply/Demand in 1985 (millions of barrels per day)

	Source of Forecast			
	Chase Manhattan Bank	Stanford Research Institute	National Petroleum Council	Shell Oil Company
Oil Demand	30.2	31.0	25.8	30.5
Oil Supply	15.0	14.0	12.3	10.5
Deficit	15.2	17.0	13.5	20.0

Table 5-3. Average Gulf Coast Cargo Prices, 1970-1975 (¢/gallon)

Year	Regular Gasoline	Jet Grade Kerosene	Diesel Fuel	Home Heating Oil	Heavy (Utility) Fuel Oil
1970	10.6	—	9.6	9.4	5.8
1971	11.1	—	9.8	9.8	6.7
1972	11.7	10.6	10.1	10.1	4.9
1973	19.5	22.2	21.7	21.7	8.2
1974	35.7	32.2	30.8	29.8	24.5

Source: *Platt's Oil Price Handbook*, 51st ed., 1975.

Figure 5-2. Demand/Supply Projections for All Forms of Energy to 1985

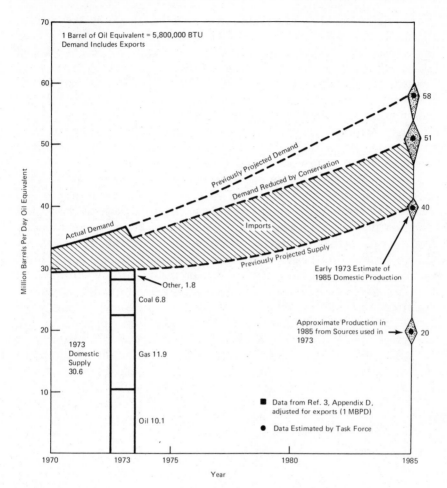

Source: National Academy of Engineering, "U.S. Energy Prospects," May 1974.

CONCLUSION

A rational assessment of any proposed policy, including the current proposals embodied in the Interfuel Competition Act, requires that the prospective social gains be weighed against prospective social losses. Since in any rank ordering of important industries by concentration levels the oil industry falls in the bottom half of the list, and considerably below the average for all manufacturing, the case for remedial measures in the form of further deconcentration through divestiture is without economic merit. The social gains from divestiture, as measured by the conventional tools of economic analysis, would appear at best to be extremely small.

On the other hand, the evidence suggests that the social costs as measured in terms of prospective lost price competition, capital availability, the development of energy sources, and technological progress may be significant. And while there are no means readily available for attaching precise quantities to these costs, it is apparent that a serious conflict exists between a national policy that on one hand assigns a high priority to the provision of low-cost energy supplies to consumers and the accelerated development of energy resources to achieve energy self-sufficiency, while on the other hand seeks large-scale dismemberment of precisely those operations that are most likely to bring these objectives about. Consistency in national policies may not be the highest of public virtues, but demonstrable conflicts should at least be recognized and hopefully resolved in the public interest.

Appendix A

Non-Petroleum Energy Patents and Patent Holders

In order to develop hard, impartial data reflecting R&D activities in synthetic fuels, the 12-year index to *Synthetic Fuels* and its predecessor, *Oil Shale and Related Fuels*, both published by Cameron Engineers, Inc. (an independent engineering and engineering consulting firm),[a] were examined for patents granted in the areas of coal conversion and oil shale processing during the period 1964-1975.

In order to determine the technology involved in the patents, the number of claims, and the assignee referred to in the *Synthetic Fuel* index, the actual patents were examined. Patents are organized according to class and subclass. Oil shale patents falls into patent class 208 (subclass 11); coal conversion patents fall into class 201 (subclass 25 and 35), class 48 (subclass 210), and class 208 (subclass 8 and 9). Each patent from 1964 to 1975 was examined to see if the technology described was specifically related to oil shale and coal conversion. If it was, it was included in the study. Tabulation of the results of this examination follow.

---

[a]Cameron Engineers, Inc., 1315 South Clarkson St., Denver, Colorado 80210.

Table A-1. Coal Conversion Patents Summary Sheet

Type of Company	Total Number of Patents	Percent of Total[a]	Number of Companies	Total Number of Claims[b]	Percent of Total[a]
Petroleum Companies	29	46.0%	8	344	53.6%
Process Contractors and Engineering Companies	18	28.5	3	165	25.7
Associations, Institutes, Research Organizations	3	4.7	1	21	3.2
Coal Companies[c]	6	9.5	2	40	6.2
U.S. Government	5	7.9	N/A	58	9.0
Unclassified Companies	2	3.2	2	14	2.2
Totals	63	100.0	16	642	100.0

[a]Individual percentages may not add to totals due to rounding.

[b]The number of claims refers to the number of individual processes or parts involved in a patent.

[c]Of the six patents granted to coal companies, three were granted to Consolidation Coal after its acquisition by Conoco.

Source: Cameron Engineers, *Synthetic Fuels* and *Oil Shale and Related Fuels* 1964-1975; U.S. Patent Office, Class 201 (subclasses 25 and 35), Class 48 (subclass 210), Class 208 (subclasses 8 and 9).

Table A-2. Petroleum Companies Summary Sheet: Patents Relating To Coal Conversion

Company	Number of Patents	Number of Claims
Exxon	10	113
Atlantic Richfield	4	24
Kerr-McGee	4	106
Sun Oil	3	18
Texaco	3	21
Ashland	1	10
Cities Service	1	9
Gulf	1	23
Totals	31	367

Table A-3. Coal Conversion Patents

I. Petroleum Companies

	Company	Claims	Type of Patent	Year
1.	Gulf	20	Solvation process	1967
2.	Exxon	12	Hydrogenation of coal	1970
3.	Exxon	14	Catalytic hydrogenation of coal	1970
4.	Atlantic Richfield	3	Producing synthetic crude from coal	1970
5.	Atlantic Richfield	8	Producing synthetic crude from coal	1970
6.	Ashland	10	Jet fuel from blended conversion products	1970
7.	Texaco	6	Purification of petroleum coke	1971
8.	Sun Oil	6	Coal hydrogenation	1971
9.	Kerr-McGee	30	Coal solvation & hydrogenation	1971
10.	Sun Oil	4	Thermal liquefaction of coal	1971
11.	Kerr-McGee	31	Coal liquefaction	1971
12.	Kerr-McGee	28	Fractionating coal liquefaction	1971
13.	Cities Service	9	Method for recovering of coal energy	1971
14.	Exxon	9	Coal liquefaction	1972
15.	Kerr-McGee	17	Solvation of coal in by-product streams	1972
16.	Sun Oil	8	Coal dissolution process	1972
17.	Atlantic Richfield	7	Coal hydrogenation	1972
18.	Atlantic Richfield	6	Coal hydrogenation	1972
19.	Texaco	8	Multihydrotorting process	1973
20.	Exxon	11	Integrated coal liquefaction & hydrotreating process	1973
21.	Exxon	14	Coal liquefaction using high & low boiling solvent	1973
22.	Exxon	17	Cokeless coker with recycle of coke	1974
23.	Exxon	4	Process for activating carbonaceous materials	1974
24.	Texaco	7	Formation reduction in pressure coking equipment	1974
25.	Exxon	12	Coal liquefaction solids removal	1974
26.	Exxon	10	Coal conversion process	1974
27.	Exxon	10	Residium packing	1974

II. Process Contractors & Engineering Companies

1.	Lummus Company	8	Deashing coal in absence of added hydrogen	1968
2.	Universal Oil Products	4	Liquefaction of coal	1969
3.	Universal Oil Products	8	Liquefaction of coal	1970
4.	Universal Oil Products	7	Coal liquefaction	1970
5.	Universal Oil Products	3	Coal liquefaction	1970
6.	Universal Oil Products	6	Coal liquefaction	1970
7.	Universal Oil Products	10	Solvent extraction method	1970

Company	Claims	Type of Patent	Year
8. Universal Oil Products	7	Coal liquefaction	1970
9. Universal Oil Products	5	Coal liquefaction	1970
10. Universal Oil Products	4	Coal liquefaction	1970
11. Universal Oil Products	4	Coal liquefaction	1970
12. Universal Oil Products	18	Coal liquefaction	1971
13. Universal Oil Products	5	Coal liquefaction	1971
14. Bechtel International	5	Coal liquefaction	1974
15. Lummus Company	14	Coal liquefaction	1974
16. Lummus Company	8	Coal liquefaction	
17. Lummus Company	31	Coal liquefaction	1974
18. Lummus Company	18	Desulphurizing coke using a ferruginous material and chloride metal	1975

III. Associations, Institutes, Research Organizations

1. Hydrocarbon Research	5	Fractional vapor product absorption	1968
2. Hydrocarbon Research	9	Hydrogenation of coal	1971
3. Hydrocarbon Research	7	Solids removal from hydrogenated coal liquids	1973

IV. Coal Companies

1. Consolidation Coal	5	Production of hydrogen-rich liquid fuels	1964
2. Consolidation Coal	3	Process for producing hydrogen enriched hydrocarbons from coal	1965
3. Consolidation Coal	15	Conversion of coal by solvent extraction	1973
4. Consolidation Coal	2	Conversion of coal to clean fuel	1974
5. Midway Coal & Mining	11	Process for refining carbonaceous fuels	1974
6. Consolidation Coal	4	Process for making liquid & gaseous fuels from coking coals	1975

V. U.S. Government

1. U.S. Government	5	Copyrolysis of coal	1974
2. U.S. Government	12	Two-stage gasification of coal	1974
3. U.S. Government	8	In-situ coal bed gasification	1974
4. U.S. Government	18	Solvent refined coal process	1975
5. U.S. Government	15	Dual temperature coal solvation	1975

VI. Unclassified Companies

1. Leas Bros. Dev. Corp.	9	Production of pollution-free fuels	1973
2. Total Energy Corp.	5	Hydrocracking of coal liquids	1974

Table A-4. Oil Shale Patents Summary Sheet

Type of Company	Total Number of Patents	Percent of Total[a]	Number of Companies	Total Number of Claims[b]	Percent of Total[a]
Petroleum Companies	69	80.2%	18	656	78.5%
Manufacturing and Engineering Companies	8	9.0%	6	85	10.1%
Associations, Institutes, Research Organizations	6	7.0%	4	62	7.4%
Unclassified Companies	3	3.5%	3	36	4.3%
Totals	86	100.0%	31	839	100.0%

[a]Individual percentages may not add to totals due to rounding.

[b]The number of claims refers to the number of individual processes or parts involved in a patent.

Source: Cameron Engineers, *Synthetic Fuels* and *Oil Shale and Related Fuels*, 1964-1975; U.S. Patent Office, Class 208 (subclass 11).

Table A-5. Patents Relating to Oil Shale Processing: Petroleum Companies Summary Sheet

Company	Number of Patents	Number of Claims
Atlantic Richfield	10	203
Exxon	9	74
Mobil	8	55
Oil Shale Corp.	7	98
Texaco	7	46
Phillips Petroleum	6	30
Shell	5	23
Paraho Corporation	2	32
Cities Service	2	21
Continental Oil	2	8
Pan American Petroleum	2	7
Sinclair	2	2
Union Oil	2	31
Chevron	1	1
Standard Oil of Ohio	1	3
Signal Oil & Gas	1	4
Standard Oil–Indiana	1	12
Sun Oil	1	6
Totals	69	656

Table A-6. Oil Shale Processing Patents

I. Petroleum Companies

	Company	Claims	Type of Patent	Year
1.	Texaco	3	Recovery of oil from shale	1964
2.	Standard Oil of Ohio	3	Oil from oil bearing minerals	1964
3.	Exxon	3	Shale distillation/retorting	1964
4.	Oil Shale Corp.	17	Transport of balls by oil	1964
5.	Texaco	7	Recovery of oil from oil shale	1965
6.	Oil Shale Corp.	21	Production of oil from solid carbon-aceous materials	1965
7.	Union Oil	20	Oil shale retorting with oil shale recycle	1966
8.	Cities Service	11	Geochemical method of soil surveying	1966
9.	Signal Oil & Gas	4	Fluidizing procedure for oil recovery	1966
10.	Mobil Oil	3	Separating & cracking shale oil from oil shale	1966
11.	Oil Shale Corp.	22	Treating oil derived by thermal treatment	1966
12.	Exxon	10	Retorting bituminous solids	1967
13.	Mobil Oil	10	Retorting of oil shale	1967
14.	Mobil Oil	9	Method & apparatus for retorting oil shale	1967
15.	Union Oil	11	Shale retorting process	1968
16.	Exxon	9	Oil shale retorting	1968
17	Shell Oil	3	Recovery of hydrocarbons	1968
18.	Chevron	1	Shale retorting apparatus	1968
19.	Exxon	6	Retorting of oil shale	1969
20.	Sun Oil	6	Tunnel oven for gaseous treatment of solid materials	1969
21.	Pan American Petroleum	5	Oil shale retorting method	1969
22.	Exxon	8	Oil shale retorting	1969
23.	Phillips Petroleum	5	Oil shale combustion	1969
24.	Continental Oil	4	In-situ retorting of oil shale using CO_2	1969
25.	Mobil	5	Traveling grate shale retorting	1969
26.	Exxon	7	Fluidized retorting of oil shale	1969
27.	Pan American Petroleum	2	Catalytic oxidation in oil shale retorting	1969
28.	Exxon	10	Retorting total raw shale	1970
29.	Phillips Petroleum	3	Process for treating crushed oil shale	1970
30.	Phillips Petroleum	7	Retorting of hydrocarbonaceous solids	1970
31.	Mobil	4	Gas lift retorting process	1970
32.	Mobil	4	Thermal efficiency of gas combustion shale retorting	1970
33.	Sinclair	15	Recovery of oil & aluminum from shale	1970
34.	Exxon	10	Retorting of oil shale	1970
35.	Shell	1	Simultaneous pipeline transportation and recovery of oil from shale	1970
36.	Sinclair	13	Hydrovisbreaking & deasphalting shale oil	1970

	Company	Claims	Type of Patent	Year
37.	Phillips Petroleum	3	Conversion of oil shale retorting gases	1970
38.	Oil Shale Corporation	16	Apparatus & method for retorting solids	1970
39.	Phillips Petroleum	5	Process for retorting oil shale	1971
40.	Phillips Petroleum	7	Recovery & conversion of shale oil mist	1971
41.	Mobil	4	Liquid disengaging system	1971
42.	Standard Oil–Indiana	12	Pyrolosis & catalytic hydrogenation	1971
43.	Texaco	8	Hydrotorting shale to produce shale oil	1971
44.	Exxon	11	Retorting of oil shale	1971
45.	Mobil	16	Method & apparatus for retorting oil shale	1971
46.	Atlantic Richfield	8	Gas combustion retort process	1971
47.	Atlantic Richfield	7	Process for recovering volatile materials from solid carbonaceous material	1971
48.	Atlantic Richfield	20	Process for recovering volatile materials from solid carbonaceous material	1971
49.	Texaco	2	Recovering oil shale	1971
50.	Texaco	11	Recovering oil shale	1971
51.	Texaco	8	Hydroretorting of oil shale	1971
52.	Texaco	7	Retorting with synthesis gas	1971
53.	Continental Oil	4	Gas retorting system	1971
54.	Oil Shale Corporation	9	Retorting oil shale	1971
55.	Shell	6	Retorting oil bearing shale	1972
56.	Atlantic Richfield	8	Catalytic cracking of shale oil	1972
57.	Shell	6	Halogenating extraction of oil from shale	1972
58.	Oil Shale Corporation	5	Retorting oil shale in absence of shale ash	1972
59.	Paraho Corporation	17	Retorting of solid carbonaceous material	1973
60.	Cities Service	10	Processing & apparatus for oil shale retorting	1974
61.	Atlantic Richfield	24	Separating retorted shale from recycled heat carrying pellets	1974
62.	Atlantic Richfield	3	Retorting system	1974
63.	Atlantic Richfield	25	Retorting oil shale in special heat carriers	1974
64.	Paraho Corporation	15	Retorting method	1974
65.	Atlantic Richfield	43	Retorting oil shale with special pellets & supplemental deposition	1974
66.	Atlantic Richfield	25	Retorting oil shale with special pellets	1974
67.	Atlantic Richfield	40	Retorting oil shale with special pellets & steam stripping	1974
68.	Oil Shale Corporation	8	Preheating oil shale prior to pyrolysis	1975
69.	Shell	8	Pipeline processing	1975

II. Manufacturing & Engineering Companies

	Company	Claims	Type of Patent	Year
1.	Cameron & Jones	5	Treating & pipelining crude shale oil-coal slurries	1964

Company	Claims	Type of Patent	Year
2. Pullman	6	Method deaeration	1964
3. Koppers Company	10	Oil shale retorting method & apparatus	1970
4. Allis-Chalmers	3	Traveling grate method for recovery of oil from shale	1971
5. Allis-Chalmers	3	Retorting oil shale including agglomerated fires	
6. Allis-Chalmers	1	Recovery of oil from shale by indirect heating	1972
7. Universal Oil Products	20	Moving bed reactor conversion	1975
8. McDowell-Wellman	37	Traveling grate method for recovery of oil	1967

III. Associations, Institutes, Research Organizations

Company	Claims	Type of Patent	Year
1. Hydrocarbon Research	3	Suspension hydrogenation of heavy stocks	1964
2. National Research Council (Canada)	10	Oil phase separation	1968
3. Instiute of Gas Technology	4	Free fuel shale hydrogasification	1969
4. Hydrocarbon Research	10	Production of hydrocarbons from shale	1969
5. Institute of Gas Technology	17	Process for production of pipeline quality gas from oil shale	1972
6. American Gas Association	18	Process for production of hydrocarbon liquids & gas from shale oil	1975

IV. Unclassified Companies

Company	Claims	Type of Patent	Year
1. Pyrochem Corporation	4	Contact catalysis	1966
2. Technikoil	23	Pyrolizing solid carbonaceous material	1966
3. Petrolite Corporation	9	Shale oil purification	1975

Appendix B

Energy Activities of Petroleum Companies by Size Group

Table B-1. Comparison of U.S. Petroleum, Coal, Uranium Concentrate, and Geothermal Energy Production by Top Eight Ranked Domestic Petroleum Producers, 1974

	Petroleum			Coal			Uranium			Geothermal		
	Petroleum Liquids Produced (MB/D)[a]	% of Total Petroleum Liquids Produced (%)	Petroleum Liquids Producer Rank	Coal Production (M Tons)	% of Total Coal Produced (%)	Coal Producer Rank	Uranium Concentrate Production (Tons)	% of Total Uranium Concentrate Produced (%)	Uranium Concentrate Producer Rank	Geothermal Energy Production (M Kilowatts)	% of Total Geothermal Energy Produced (%)	Geothermal Energy Producer Rank
Exxon	890	8.5%	1	2,480	0.4%	37	850	7.4%	5	–	–	–
Texaco	705	6.7	2	–	–	–	–	–	–	–	–	–
Shell Oil	586	5.6	3	–	–	–	–	–	–	–	–	–
Std. of Indiana	539	5.2	4	–	–	–	–	–	–	–	–	–
Gulf	476	4.6	5	7,528	1.3	13	–	–	–	–	–	–
Std. of California	413	4.0	6	–	–	–	–	–	–	–	–	–
ARCO	383	3.7	7	–	–	–	–	–	–	–	–	–
Mobil	363	3.5	8	–	–	–	–	–	–	–	–	–
Total, Top 8	4,355	41.7	N/A	10,028	1.7	N/A	850	7.4	N/A	–	–	–

[a]Net crude oil, condensate, and natural gas liquids.

Sources: Petroleum: FTC, Concentration Levels and Trends in the Energy Sector of the U.S. Economy, 1974; Coal: Keystone News Bulletin, February 20 and March 25, 1975, and corporate annual reports; Uranium: House Committee on Mines and Mining.

Table B-2. Comparison of U.S. Petroleum, Coal, Uranium Concentrate, and Geothermal Energy Production by Domestic Petroleum Producers Ranked 9-20, 1974

	Petroleum			Coal			Uranium			Geothermal		
	Petroleum Liquids Produced (MB/D)[a]	% of Total Petroleum Liquids Produced %	Petroleum Liquids Produced Rank	Coal Production (M Tons)	% of Total Coal Produced (%)	Coal Producer Rank	Uranium Concentrate Production (Tons)	% of Total Concentrate Produced	Uranium Concentrate Producer Rank	Geothermal Energy Production (Thousand Kilowatts)	% of Total Geothermal Energy Produced (%)	Geothermal Energy Producer Rank
Getty	300	2.9%	9	—	—	—	—	—	—	—	—	—
Union	268	2.6	10	—	—	—	—	—	—	—	—	—
Sun	266	2.5	11	—	—	—	—	—	—	390	100%	1
Phillips	256	2.4	12	—	—	—	—	—	—	—	—	—
Continental	218	2.1	13	51,800	8.6%	2	—	—	—	—	—	—
Cities Service	212	2.0	14	—	—	—	481	4.2%	9	—	—	—
Marathon	174	1.7	15	—	—	—	—	—	—	—	—	—
Amerada Hess	99	0.9	16	—	—	—	—	—	—	—	—	—
Tennaco	88	0.8	17	—	—	—	—	—	—	—	—	—
Louisiana Land	77	0.7	18	—	—	—	—	—	—	—	—	—
Superior	60	0.6	19	—	—	—	—	—	—	—	—	—
Pennzoil	54	0.5	20	—	—	—	—	—	—	—	—	—
Total Petroleum Producers Ranked 9-20	2,070	19.7	N/A	51,800	8.6	N/A	481	4.2	N/A	390	100	N/A

[a]Net crude oil, condensate, and natural gas liquids.

Sources: Petroleum: FTC, *Concentration Levels and Trends in the Energy Sector of the U.S. Economy,* 1974; Coal: *Keystone News Bulletin,* February 26 and March 25, 1976, and corporate annual reports; Uranium: House Committee on Mines and Mining; Geothermal: corporate annual reports.

Table B-3. Comparison of U.S. Petroleum, Coal, Uranium Concentrate, and Geothermal Energy Production by Small Domestic Petroleum Producers, 1974

	Petroleum			Coal			Uranium			Geothermal		
	Petroleum Liquids Produced (MB/D)[a]	% of Total Petroleum Liquids Produced (%)	Petroleum Liquids Producer Rank	Coal Production (M Tons)	% of Total Coal Production (%)	Coal Producer Rank	Uranium Concentrate Production (Tons)	% of Total Concentrate Produced	Uranium Concentrate Producer Rank	Geothermal Energy Production (Thousand Kilowatts)	% of Total Geothermal Energy Produced (%)	Geothermal Energy Producer Rank
Std. of Ohio	30	0.3%	—[b]	9,500	1.6%	10	—	—	—	—	—	—
Kerr-McGee	37	.4	—[b]	—	—	—	1,800	15.8%	1	—	—	—
Occidental Pet.	8	.1	—[b]	20,800	3.5	3	—	—	—	—	—	—
Belco	14	.1	—[b]	1,300	0.2	61	—	—	—	—	—	—
Ashland	22	.2	—[b]	13,900	2.3	8	—	—	—	—	—	—
Quaker State	4	.0	—[b]	3,295	0.5[c]	28	—	—	—	—	—	—
Total Small Petroleum Producers	115	1.1		48,795	8.1		1,800	15.8		—	—	—

[a]Net crude, condensate and natural gas liquids.

[b]Not computed, very minor production.

[c]On March 8, 1976 Quaker State reached an agreement in principle with the Valley Camp Coal Company for Quaker State to acquire Valley Camp. The data shown for coal production reflects Valley Camp's production in 1974.

Sources: Petroleum: corporate annual reports; Coal: *Keystone News Bulletin*, February 26 and March 25, 1975, and corporate annual reports; Uranium: House Committee on Mines and Mining.

Appendix C

Continental Oil Company: Research and Engineering Interactions

The following specific cases of research and engineering interactions would probably not occur if the researchers were separated by either horizontal or vertical divestitures. The arrow by each item is intended to indicate the flow of technology using the following key:

E — Petroleum Exploration
P — Petroleum Production
R — Petroleum Refining
T — Transportation
M — Mining
C — Chemicals
CC — Coal Conversion

thus, by item 1, the $T \to M$ is intended to indicate the use of transportation technology in coal mining.

$T \longrightarrow M$ Use of pipeline technology in developing the new hydraulic transportation coal mining system.

$C \longrightarrow P$ Use of petrochemical surfactant technology on tertiary recovery processes.

$C \longrightarrow P$ Use of petrochemical surfactant technology on "adomite"—fluid-loss control additive for drilling fluids.

$C \longrightarrow R$ Use of petrochemical surfactant technology in development of detergent-type lubricating oil additives.

$R \longrightarrow C$ and $R \longrightarrow P$

Use of overbasing lube oil additive technology in preparation of corrosion preventative coating (SACI), and metal containing spectroscopic standards (CONO-STAN) and overbased tertiary recovery surfactants.

$E \longrightarrow M$ Use of "VIBROSEIS" technology in location of flooded-out mine tunnels.

$P \longrightarrow M$ Use of oilfield drilling technology in developing pilot hole drilling in coal.

$P \longrightarrow M$ Use of oilfield technology in production of methane by degassing of coal prior to mining and recovery of gas from "gob" area after mining.

$\begin{matrix} C \\ P \end{matrix} \!\!\! \begin{matrix} \searrow \\ \nearrow \end{matrix} CC$ Use of chemical and gas production technologies in demonstration of methanation at Westfield, Scotland.

$E \longrightarrow M$ Use of seismograph knowledge in developing systems for location of trapped miners.

$P \longrightarrow C$ Use of microbiological oilfield technology in development of biodegradable detergents.

$C \longrightarrow R$ Use of by-products from biodegradable detergent manufacture in production of arctic synthetic lubricants.

$C \longrightarrow T$ Use of polyurethane foam technology (petrochemical and plastic) in developing insulation system for LNG transportation.

$C \longrightarrow R$ Use of alumina from petrochemical operations in catalyst supports for refining dehydrosulfurization catalysts and automobile catalytic converters.

$E \longrightarrow M$ Use of oilfield geological technology in developing methods for location of uranium deposits.

$C \longrightarrow E$ Use of petrochemical analytical technique (nuclear magnetic resonance) to find stable free radicals in shale samples and thereby determine maximum paleo-temperature of a formation.

$R \searrow \atop C \nearrow CC$ Utilization of all of the refining and petrochemical design, construction, and particularly maintenance engineering technology and know-how at Westfield, Scotland and Rapid City, South Dakota on coal gasification pilot plants and at Cresap, West Virginia on coal liquefaction pilot plant.

$\begin{array}{c} R \\ \nearrow \nwarrow \\ M \leftrightarrow C \end{array}$ Exchange of maintenance and construction engineering know-how between the coal company and the oil company.

$C \longrightarrow P$ Utilization of automatic analytical techniques originally developed for petrochemical research in the research work on tertiary oil recovery.

$C \langle{R \atop P}$ Use of microbiological techniques from degradable detergent development in land farming for disposal of oily wastes from refining and oil production.

$R \longrightarrow M$ Utilization of critical path scheduling experience from "refinery turn-around" on coal processing plants and coal mine construction.

$P \longrightarrow M$ Use of oilfield microbiological techniques on acid drainage problems from coal mines.

$P \longrightarrow M$ Use of oilfield reservoir technology on slurry and/or solution mining and in-situ leaching of minerals, including potash, phosphates, and uranium.

$M \longrightarrow R$ Use of boiler room technical experience in providing alternative fuels for utilities.

$C \longrightarrow P$ Utilization of plastics knowledge in producing a rough surface for a cement bond on oilwell casing.

$C \longrightarrow M$ Use of chemical processing know-how on molten salt breeder design and feasibility studies.

$C \longrightarrow R$ Use of plastics knowledge in producing wax coatings for paper curtain-coating and for wet-strength boxes.

$P \longrightarrow C$ Use of oilfield corrosion information on metal activation in preparation of aluminum alkyls.

$\begin{array}{c} P \leftrightarrow M \\ \updownarrow \times \updownarrow \\ R \leftrightarrow C \end{array}$ Use of basic metallurgical information throughout all operations.

Use of environmental conservation technology by all operations.

$E \longrightarrow M$ Use of oilfield geophysical technology in minerals exploration.

✳ *Appendix D*

The Status of Synthetic
Fuel Projects

SYNTHETIC FUELS FROM OIL SHALE

COMMERCIAL PROJECTS

Principals: Ashland Oil, Shell Oil Co.

Project Name: Roxana Shale Oil Co.

Project   Proposed 50,000 BPD plant on 5,094-acre federal tract C-b; Piceance Creek
Description: basin, Colo.

Details: Rights acquired on bid of $117.8 million at DOI lease sale 2/12/74.
              Lease issued 4/1/74 to the above plus Atlantic Richfield Co. and The
              Oil Shale Corp. ARCO and TOSCO announced withdrawal from project on
              12/19/75. New partners being sought. Shell Oil, operator, announced
              12/10/75 that efforts being reduced to minimum required by lease and
              development postponed at least a year.

Project Cost: Estimated at $923 million

Status: Decision on full development in doubt (See page 2-26)
              Detailed Development Plan submitted Feb. 9, '76

                                   * * *

Principals: Atlantic Richfield Co., The Oil Shale Corp., Ashland Oil, Shell Oil Co.

Project Name: Colony Development Operation

Project
Description: Proposed 50,000 BPD plant on 44,000 acres of Dow West fee land north
             of Grand Valley, Colo.

Details: Room and pillar mining of a 60-foot horizon producing 66,000 tons of
              35 GPT shale daily through TOSCO II retort system. Mining of about
              4,100 underground acres anticipated. Water requirement: 10,000 AFY.

Project Cost: Estimated at $1,132 million including $20 million for community
              development

Status: No announced change since development suspended 10/4/74. Draft EIS
              covering plant, utility corridor, 196-mile 50,000 BPD pipeline to
              LaSal, Utah, and minor land exchanges released 12/17/75. EIS required
              only for pipeline right-of-way permit. Ten environmental organizations
              filed opposition to issuance of final EIS because project suspended.
              Railroad spur completion scheduled spring '76. Revegetation, water supply,
              land exchange, and community planning efforts continuing. (See page 2-13.)

                                   * * *

_____

Underlining denotes changes since December 1975

Principals: Standard Oil of Indiana, Gulf Oil Corp.

Project Name: Rio Blanco Oil Shale Project

Project
Description: Proposed 50,000 BPD plant on 5,090-acre federal tract C-a, Piceance Creek
basin, Colo.

Details: Rights acquired on $210.3 million bid at DOI lease sale 1/8/74.
Proposed open pit mine for 25-30 GPT shale. Operational by 1979 at
11,000 BPD with later expansion to 50,000 BPD and possibly to
300,000 BPD. Water requirement for 50,000 BPD plant, 11,200 AFY;
60,000 AFY sought for potential 300,000 BPD. Recoverable reserves
4 billion BBL open pit; 1.3 billion BBl underground. Off-tract
surface site sought for spent shale disposal.

Project Cost: First module of TOSCO II plant and some support facilities, $160 million;
50,000 BD plant on line in 1985, $1 billion 1976 dollars not including
lease payments and environmental studies.

Status: DDP due March '76. House and Senate Interior Committees considering
bills authorizing DOI to lease surface rights for disposal. BLM approval
of utility corridor from Rangely including Moon Lake Electric power line
route pending.

* * *

Principals: Sun Oil Co., Phillips Petroleum Corp.

Project Name: Utah federal prototype lease U-a

Project
Description: Proposed 50,000 BPD plant in conjunction with tract U-b, Uintah County, Utah.

Details: Rights acquired on $76.6 million bid 3/12/74. Lease let 6/1/74. Room and
pillar mining of 30 GPT shales at rate of 80,000 TPD from 50-60 foot
horizon about 1,300 feet underground. Both TOSCO II and Paraho retorting
anticipated with Paraho processing 80 percent of mine production. Water
requirement 8,250 AFY. Water development contract in negotiation with state.
Construction labor, 1,350; permanent force of 850. Joint development with
adjacent U-b under advisement by DOI. Reserve estimated at 244 million BBL.
Modular development planned.

Project Cost: Estimated to exceed $600 million

Status: DDP to be filed in March '76. Water assurances imminent with state backing.

* * *

Principal: White River Shale Oil Corp. (Sun, Phillips and Sohio)

Project Name: Federal prototype lease U-b

Project
Description: Proposed 50,000 BPD plant in conjunction with tract U-a, Uintah County, Utah

Details: Rights on 5,120-acre tract acquired with $45.1 million bid 4/9/74. Lease
issued 6/1/74. Recoverable reserves estimated at 266 million barrels. Room
and pillar mining, processing by Paraho retort probable. By-product of shale
crushing briquetted for Paraho, or processed in TOSCO II retort. White
River water development shared with U-a, Ute Indians, Uinta and Central Utah
water districts, Bureau of Reclamation.

Project Cost: Expected to exceed $600 million

Status: Environmental exploratory work underway. DDP to be filed March '76. Water
development with state help imminent (see page 2-9 and 2-48 in Sept. 75 issue).

* * *

Principal: Superior Oil Co

Project
Description: Proposed 50,000 BPD shale and sodium mineral development on 7,000 acres of
private land west of Meeker, Colorado

Details: Mining of 80,000 TPD of 25 GPT shale to yield 50,000 BB shale oil; 5,000
to 15,000 TPD nahcolite; 3,000 TPD aluminum trihydrate (or 2,300 TPD alumina);
and 3,000 TPD soda ash from underground mine. Underground ore processing
for surface pyrolization in continual feed, circular, traveling grate retort.
Application to Interior for exchange of 2,571 acres Superior land for
1,769 adjacent BLM acres to block up economical unit filed 12/3/73. Spent

shale backfilled in mine. Employment 1,000. Recovery of multiple products offers economic advantages. Completion of pilot plant work anticipated mid-1976. Various industries testing nahcolite for scrubbing of stack gasses and release of test data planned in spring 76.

Project Cost: Expected to exceed $600 million

Status: USGS completing appraisal of mineral values on lands involved in proposed exchange. Title clearance and environmental impact statement work to follow: (See page 2-53 in March 74 edition)

* * *

Principal: The Oil Shale Corp.

Project Name: Sand Wash Unit

Project
Description: Proposed 75,000 BPD plant on 14,688 acres of Utah state leases in Sand Wash area near Vernal, Utah

Details: Utah State Land Division approved unitization of 29 state shale leases totaling 14,688 acres in Sand Wash area south of Vernal. Unitization agreement requires $8 million tract evaluation by 12/31/84 with minimum per acre royalty of $5 starting in 1984 and increasing by $5 per acre annually to a minimum $50 per acre royalty in 1993. Preliminary plans are to room and pillar mine 75,000 TPD by room and piller from 30 to 40 foot interval 2,000 feet underground. Processing by TOSCO II retort.

Project Cost: About $1 billion

Status: Pre-development environmental and engineering work started (see page 2-21)

* * *

Principal: Union Oil Co., California

Project
Description: Proposed 7,000 BPD plant on 22,000 acres of private land near Grand Valley, Colo.

Details: Union proposes to use its 'B' retort for a 10,000 TPD feed of 30-35 GPT shale from a room and pillar mine on the east fork of Parachute Creek. Processing water requirement 1,500 AFY using Colorado River rights and intake structure. Eventual site scale-up to 150,000 BPD possible. High grade reserves hold 2 billion barrels. Needs favorable political and economic climate to proceed.

Project Cost: Undetermined

Status: Engineering and environmental studies substantially completed for prototype retorting facility in 10,000 TPD range. Union says it is ready to proceed with construction when federal economic support is made available and currently is holding discussions with ERDA about such support.

* * *

Principal: Occidental Oil Shale, Inc.

Project Name: Logan Wash site

Project
Description: Modified in situ shale oil recovery near DeBeque, Colorado, on D.A. shale tract

Details: Modified in situ with upper and lower level adit. 120' by 120' by 310' column of 15 GPT fractured shale ignited 12/10/75. Top of column ignited and oil recovered from sump at bottom of column. Gas recycled for sustained combustion and temperature control. Present work is scale-up from 30' by 30' by 70' results.

Project Cost: $30 million expended to date

Status: Retort burning with unspecified amount of oil being produced. No. 5 retort of similar dimensions being prepared. Garfield County Commissioners approved 1/12/76 permit for increase in mined waste disposal pile from 500,000 to 8.8 million cubic yards. (See page 2-20).

* * *

DEMONSTRATION, PILOT OR RESEARCH PROJECTS

Principal: Dow Chemical Co.

Project
Description: Proposed in situ oil and gas recovery near Midland, Mich.

Details: Dow asked ERDA for $42 million for seven-year field evaluation on extracting
                     low BTU gas and liquid products from 200 foot horizon of Antrim shales 3,000
                     feet underground. Fracturing needed prior to using forward combustion
                     process on 9 GPT shales. Reserves extensive, inasmuch of 2/3rds of state
                     is underlain with shale.

Project Cost: $42 million.

Status: ERDA evaluating proposal. No recent agency action. Laramie Energy
                     Research Center preparing to retort 300 tons of Antrim Shale in 10-ton
                     batch retort   (See page 2-7).

* * *

Principal: Geokinetics, Inc.

Project
Description: In situ test in Uintah County, Utah

Details: Test is in NE 1/4 of Section 2, T14S, R22E. Approved by Utah Board
                     of Oil, Gas and Mining on 9/17/75. Test involves explosive fracturing
                     of shallow oil shale deposits followed by in situ retorting by means
                     of horizontal fire front.

Project Cost: Not revealed

Status: Field work underway. Tight hole.

* * *

Principals: Institute of Gas Technology and American Gas Association

Project Name: IGT Project No. IU-4-7, Gasification of Oil Shale

Project
Description: One ton/hour oil shale gasification pilot plant located in Chicago

Details: Pilot plant completed late in 1975. Designed to treat 25 GPT oil shale
                     from Anvil Points mine in Colorado in one ton/hour non-continuous feed
                     tests. Tests of 8 and 10-hour duration planned to verify bench-scale
                     yields of up to 80 per cent conversion of organic carbon to gaseous
                     products.

Project Cost: $350,000

Status: Start-up difficulties encountered were of a mechanical design nature.
                     Modifications being made, with completion now scheduled for March '76.

* * *

Principal: MECCO, Englewood, Colorado

Project
Description: In situ oil shale project in Uintah County, Utah

Details: MECCO has applied to the Utah Oil, Gas and Mining Board for permit to
                     conduct test on state lease in Section 16, T9S, R25E, SLM, northeast
                     of Bonanza, Utah. Test would involve drilling 12 to 32 wells on half-
                     acre test site, injection of small amount of fuel and oxidant, and burn
                     underground in a manner similar to a fireflood operation. All retorting
                     at least 200 feet underground.

Status: Awaiting permit from state. Unsolicited proposals offered to industry.

* * *

Principals: National Science Foundation, Denver Research Institute

Project
Description: DRI study of environmental effects of spent shales

Details: Study of carbonaceous solid wastes from commercial oil shale operations.
                     First annual report of 2-year study 1/75 cited properties of polynuclear/
                     polycondensed aromatics and other constituents, including carcinogenic
                     potential.

Project Cost: $120,000 NSF grant

Status: Second phase report in preparation. Proposal submitted to NSF for new grant to continue and extend study to spent shales from other processes. Work to date has concentrated on spent shale from TOSCO II process.

* * *

Principals: National Science Foundation, University of Southern California

Project
Description: Use of bacteria to release kerogen from shale

Details: Investigation by USC researcher of sulfur-oxidizing bacteria for releasing kerogen from in situ shale bodies.

Study Cost: $120,000 NSF grant

Status: Investigation completed. Final report in preparation.

* * *

Principals: Paraho Development Corp. (Development Engineering, Inc.), A. G. McKee, Arco, Carter Oil, Chevron, Cleveland Cliffs, Gulf, Kerr-McGee, Marathon, Mobil, Phillips, Shell, Sohio, Southern California Edison, Amoco, Texaco, Webb Resources

Project Name: Paraho Project

Project
Description: Development of direct/indirect retorting processes at Anvil Points Oil Shale Research Center near Rifle

Details: Direct combustion of 30 GPT shale attained up to 95 per cent recovery; 8,420 SCF of low BTU gas per ton. Operating factor 88 per cent. Low organic content in spent shale in 56 day test run.

Project Cost: $9 million

Status: Operation on indirect heating mode started 1/11/76 and was to continue through 2/18/76 at which time decision to be made on operation by combination mode. Conclusion of 30-month demonstration project scheduled for late May 1976.

* * *

Principal: Paraho Development Corp.

Project
Description: Scale-up of Paraho retort to 42-foot-diameter retort capable of processing 11,500 TPD of 30 GPT shales to yield 7,300 BPD liquids at Anvil Points. A scale-up of 8 1/2' diameter retort.

Project Cost: $53 million for construction, $23 million for 2 1/2-year test program

Status: Preparation of EIS in progress, completion expected in late 1976. Site lease extended to 1982. Participants being sought. ERDA evaluating proposal for government participation.

* * *

Principal: Petrobras (Petroleo Brasileiro, S.A.)

Project
Description: Demonstration plant near Sao Mateus do SUL, Parana, Brazil

Details: Petrosix 2,200 TPD shale retort operating near design capacity to yield 1,000 BPD oil 12 MMCF gas and 14 TPD sulfur in series of demonstration tests. Cost of production about $9 per barrel. U.S. patent obtained on the process.

Status: 50,000 BPD plant being contemplated by Mines & Energy Ministry

* * *

Principal   The Oil Shale Corp. (TOSCO)

Project
Description: Direct gasification of oil shale at research center near Denver

Details: Series of tests with 5 TPD retort using 36 GPT shales and oxygen-steam
               gasification in fluidized bed. Preliminary results warrant continued
               work.

Status: In progress

* * *

Principals: U.S. Bureau of Mines, Cameron Engineers, Inc.

Project
Description: Underground mining research studies

Details: Technical phase of 18 month study completed July 1975. Contract
               modified to include detailed development plan for underground oil
               shale mine in addition to second phase economic analysis of technology
               for mining deep, thick bedded shale deposits of Piceance Basin,
               Colorado.

Status: DDP due March 15; economic study due July 1976

Study Cost: $340,391 modified contract

* * *

Principals: U.S. Bureau of Mines, Fenix & Scisson, Inc.

Project
Description: Modified in situ oil shale study of Piceance Creek basin

Details: Study of modified in situ shale oil recovery from deep, thick bedded
               shales of Piceance Creek basin, Colorado. Features conventional mining,
               rubbilization of shales and in situ retorting. An 18-month study
               from July 1, 1974.

Project Cost: $220,696

Status: Technical phase completed. Preliminary report on economic analysis
               due for release about March 1, 76. Modification and extension of
               contract under consideration.

* * *

Principals: U.S. Bureau of Mines, Sun Oil Co.

Project
Description: Study of open pit mining of deep oil shale deposits

Details: Technical and economic analysis of open pit shale mines in Piceance Creek
               basin of Colorado. Two-year study due June 1976. Concept is for one
               large mine to supply several retorts.

Project Cost: $395,309

Status: First phase completed April, 1975; second phase underway

* * *

Principals: Western Oil Shale Corp., Ashland, Chevron, Cities Service, Getty,
               Gulf, AMOCO, Shell, Sun, A. G. McKee

Project
Description: Experimental in situ project in Uintah County, Utah

Details: Planning and costing of three small in situ chimneys in 30 GPT and
               15 GPT shales fractured by Dupont-designed explosives begun July, 1975.

Project Cost: First phase, $400,000

Status: Final report in preparation. Decision on second phase field testing
               expected in spring with field work planned by mid 1976.

* * *

SYNTHETIC FUELS FROM OIL SANDS

COMMERCIAL PROJECTS

Principals: AOP Group owned jointly by Petrofina Canada (35%), Pacific Petroleum (35%),
               Hudson Bay Oil and Gas Co., Ltd. (19%), and Murphy Oil Co., (11%)

Project
Description: Commercial plant in Athabasca bituminous sands area, Alberta, Canada

Details: Proposed plant to be located on Lease Nos. 12 and 34. Allowable production will be 122,500 BPCD. Mining - bucketwheel excavators; extraction - hot water process; upgrading - fluid coking. On-site power plant will use by-product coke. Initial production scheduled for 1982.

Project Cost: Estimated at $1.7 billion

Status: ERCB approval granted; awaiting provincial approval. Has recently applied for construction schedule deferral.

* * *

Principal: Great Canadian Oil Sands, Ltd. owned by Sun Oil Co. (97%) and publicly (3%)

Project
Description: Commercial plant in Athabasca bituminous sands area, Alberta, Canada

Details: Plant has been in operation since 1967 on Lease No. 86. Authorized annual production is 65,000 BPCD equivalent. Mining - bucketwheel excavators; extraction - hot water process; upgrading - delayed coking. Coker bottoms are used for power plant fuel. 100,000 TPY of sulfur is being exported and sold in Italy. Cumulative loss since 1968 is $85 million.

Project Cost: Undisclosed

Status: Operating

* * *

Principals: Home Oil, Ltd. and Alminex Corp.

Project
Description: Proposed commercial plant in Athabasca bituminous sands area, Alberta, Canada

Details: Proposed plant to be located on Lease No. 30. Allowable production is 103,000 BPCD. Mining - bucketwheel excavators; extraction - hot water process; upgrading - fluid coking. Initial production scheduled for 1982.

Project Cost: Estimated at $2.4 billion

Status: ERCB approval granted. Project shelved; no new development since 1974.

* * *

Principal: Shell Canada Ltd.

Project
Description: Commercial plant in Athabasca bituminous sands area, Alberta, Canada

Details: Proposed plant to be located on Lease No. 13. Allowable production is 100,000 BPCD. Mining - electric draglines; extraction - hot water process; upgrading - vacuum flash deasphalting. Initial production scheduled for 1980.

Project: $3 billion estimated

Status: ERCB approval granted. Ratification by provincial government awaited.

* * *

Principals: Syncrude Canada, Ltd., a joint venture consisting of Imperial Oil Ltd., (31.25%), Canada Cities Service Ltd. (22%), Gulf Oil Canada Ltd. (16.75%), Province of Alberta (10%), Province of Ontario (5%) and the Canadian federal government (15%)

Project
Description: Plant located on Lease No. 17. Allowable production is 125,000 BPCD. Mining - electric draglines; extraction - hot water process; upgrading - fluid coking. Canadian Bechtel, Ltd. is managing contractor. Startup scheduled for 1978 with initial production of 104,500 BPCD.

Project Cost: Estimated at more than $2 billion -- Gulf Oil Canada ($335 million), Imperial Oil ($625 million), Canada Cities Service ($440 million), the federal government ($300 million), the Alberta government $200 million), the Ontario government ($100 million).

Status: Project 25% complete; construction on schedule

* * *

DEMONSTRATION, PILOT OR RESEARCH PROJECTS

Principals: Arizona Fuels, Inc. and Burmah Oil

Project
Description: Pilot plant on Asphalt Ridge, near Vernal, Utah

Details: Plant will be located on Sohio property about 7 miles south of Vernal.
Extraction unit will be 51 feet high and 6 feet in diameter. Feed will
be loaded in the top, heated by a gas-fired furnace and bitumen will be
separated in a water filled chamber. The project will be processed at
A-F's Fredonia Arizona, refinery.

Project Cost: $3 million

Status: Start-up is scheduled for 3/1/76

* * *

Principal: AMOCO Canada Petroleum Ltd.

Project
Description: Experimental in situ recovery project in Athabasca deposit, Alberta, Canada

Details: Location is in section 27-85-8 W4M. Application submitted in October 1968
seeking provincial authority to produce 15 million barrels of crude bitumen
at rates up to 8,000 BPD. This planned sub-commercial in situ project was
to fracture the formation by the patented Hydra-Frac technique and follow up
with a combination forward combustion-water flood procedure known as the
COFCAW process. AMOCO owns patent rights to both processes.

Project Cost: Estimated at $9 million to date

Status: Expansion operations suspended. Established phases of project continuing.

* * *

Principal: Bingham Mechanical & Metal Products, Inc.

Project
Description: Pilot plant operation at Idaho Falls, Id.

Details: Pilot plant testing being conducted after 3 years of bench-scale tests on
oil sands from Asphalt Ridge, Utah. Plant to produce 2,500 BPD using cold
and solvent processes. A project bottleneck is legal problems in obtaining
process patent.

Project Cost: $1.5 million

Status: Process patent application being prepared

* * *

Principal: Canadian Javelin Ltd.

Project
Description: Pilot plant in Montreal, Canada

Details: Small scale pilot plant studies being conducted on Javelin Environmental
Protection Oil Sands System (JEPOSS). Process involves solvent extraction
after pretreatment with infrared radiation. Patent rights obtained through
Calgary subsidiary, Bison Petroleum & Minerals Ltd.

Project Cost: Undetermined

Status: Active

* * *

Principal: Chevron Standard Ltd.

Project
Description: Experimental in situ project in Cold Lake deposit, Alberta, Canada

Details: Project will be located at 36-61-2 W4 north of Imperial Oil's Lease No.39.
The one well huff-and-puff test began in July 1975. ERCB permit expires
on May 31, 1976.

Project Cost: Undetermined

Status: Active

* * *

Principal: ERDA, Laramie Energy Research Center

Project
  Description: In situ field experiment on northwest Asphalt Ridge, near Vernal, Utah

Details: The site of the reverse combustion test is five miles west of Vernal.
                The line drive pattern consists of two rows of injection wells with a
                row of producing wells between. Each row contains three wells, the rows
                are 60 feet apart and the wells in each row 20 feet apart. <u>First phase
                terminated one month after ignition on 12/23/75. Approximately 50 bbls
                of oil recovered. Experiment was shut down due to accumulation of heavy
                tars in process vessels and cold weather.</u>

Project Cost: $1 million

Status: <u>Analysis of Experimental results underway</u>

* * *

Principal: Fairbrim Company

Project
  Description: Pilot plant near Bowling Green, Kentucky

Details: A chemical extraction process is to be used, however, the exact nature of
                the chemical solvent has not been disclosed. Ore wil be obtained from local
                deposits and Ashland Oil has been contacted about the use of their facilities
                for upgrading.

Project Cost: Undetermined

Status: Active

* * *

Principal: Guardian Chemical Corp.

Project
  Description: Pilot Plant in Hauppauge, New York

Details: The project investigates the feasibility of using a low concentrate solution
                of Polycomplex to extract bitumen from oil sands. The chemical was originally
                designed to break up oil slicks. Pilot plant operates on 400#/hr of feed.
                Claim made that process uses only 1/2 the energy of conventional hot water
                process and requires only 1/3 the construction costs. Tests being made for
                interested companies. New Western Oil Sands, Ltd., a subsidiary of Rainbow
                Resources, Ltd., has provided the oil sands feed for the tests as well as
                financial backing.

Project Cost: Undetermined

Status: Pilot Plant operating

* * *

Principal: Gulf Oil Canada Ltd.

Project
  Description: Experimental in situ project in Wabasca deposit, Alberta, Canada

Details: Project will be located at 6-83-22-W4. Recovery scheme will involve the
                injection of steam through 11 wells arranged in three five-spot patterns.
                Nine observation wells will also be drilled. The producing formation lies
                at a depth of 800 ft. A 50,000 lb/hr steam generator will be installed.
                The 7° API crude product will be processed at Gulf's Calgary asphalt plant.

Project Cost: Undetermined

Status: Active

* * *

Principal: Imperial Oil, Ltd.

Project
  Description: Experimental in situ recovery project in Cold Lake deposit, Alberta, Canada

Details: Imperial has been conducting steam stimulation tests in the Ethel Lake area
                of the Cold Lake deposit since 1971. The exact location is 27-64-3 W4 on
                Imperial's Lease No. 40. In December 1973, Imperial received ERCB approval
                for production from the current project from 1,500 to 4,000 BPCD. Imperial

has sold data and ongoing program monitoring rights to five companies. New project (Leming) uses a 7-spot drilling pattern, whereas the previous project used a 5-spot pattern. Leming pilot began production in April, 1975. Fourteen well expansion is underway.

Project Cost: $5.25 million expected to be spent over the next 10 years.

Status: Active

* * *

Principal: Marconaflo, Inc. (a subsidiary of Marcona Corp.)

Project
Description: Slurry mining project in southern California

Details: Underground mining system uses high pressure water jets to remove ore and produce slurry which can be pumped to the surface. Process has been successfully used in mining uranium ores.

Project Cost: Undetermined

Status: Active

* * *

Principal: Murphy Oil Company, Ltd.

Project
Description: Experimental in situ recovery project in Cold Lake deposit, Alberta, Canada

Details: The project is located in 13-58-5 WA. Approval was granted for production of 600 BPCD. Inverted 7-spot pattern being drilled. After each hole is stimulated by huff-and-puff, steam flood will follow. Another phase is located at 11-52-4 W4, Hazeldine, is currently being steam soaked to raise reservoir temperature so as to enter huff-and-puff phase.

Project Cost: Undetermined

Status: All wells to be stimulated by end of 1976

* * *

Principals: Norcen Energy Resources Ltd., Nippon Oil Sands Co. (formerly CIGOL and Fuyo-Marubeni Oil and Gas of Alberta, Ltd.)

Project
Description: Experimental in situ project in Cold Lake deposit, Alberta, Canada

Details: Norcen will be operator of a $20 million program. A delineation drilling program is in progress on lease No. 60. If project continues as proposed, the Japanese firm will get one-half of the expected 10,000 BPCD production from 1981 to 2007.

Project Cost: $20 million total; $11,25 million by Nippon Oil Sands Co.

Status: Drilling in progress

* * *

Principal: Numac Oil and Gas Ltd.

Project
Description: Experimental in situ recovery project in Athabasca bituminous sands area, Aberta.

Details: Location is 30-83-6 W4 on Lease No. 72. The project will use a steam injection technique on a 5-spot pattern. If the pilot plant is successful, plans are to begin a commercial operation producing 100,000 BPCD.

Project Cost: Undetermined

Status: Active

* * *

Principal: Payette River Mines

Project
Description: Experimental in situ project in Duchesne County, Utah

Details: Corehole data indicates a 500 foot thick zone of oil saturated dolomite
                in Sec 12, T3S, R2W SLM. Depth is between 5,000 and 6,000 feet. Approval
                has been granted to begin hot water injection tests. The casing will be
                perforated with four perforations per foot from 5,792 to 5,800 feet and
                with two perforations per foot from 5,760 to 5,770 feet. A packer will be
                located between these intervals. Hot water will be pumped from the lower
                section in the saturation zone and up through the upper section. A ten
                foot penetration is anticipated. Success on this test could lead to huff-
                and-puff in situ techniques.

Project Cost: Undetermined

Status: Project approval granted by Utah Oil and Gas Conservation Board

* * *

Principal: Shell Canada, Ltd.

Project
 Description: Experimental in situ project in Peace River deposit, Alberta, Canada

Details: Project located at 21-85-18 W5 on Shell Lease No. 1. Program will involve
                24 production wells, 7 steam injection wells, 12 observation wells and 2
                fuel gas wells arranged in 7-spot patterns. A two-cycle steam drive process
                designed especially for the Peace River site will be used. A four-year steam
                injection phase will be followed by a 1-1/2 year production period. Possible
                large commercial scheme is being considered.

Project Cost: Total program (9-year) estimated at $85 million

Status: Experimental work terminated; ERCB permit expired 12/21/75

* * *

Principal: Tenneco Oil and Minerals

Project
 Description: Experimental in situ recovery project in Athabasca deposit, Alberta, Canada

Details: Project is located in 27-96-7 W4 on Tenneco's Lease No. 87 in the Muskeg
                River area. ERCB permit has expired. No new activity anticipated.

Status: Inactive

* * *

Principal: Texaco Exploration Canada, Ltd.

Project
 Description: Experimental in situ recovery project in Athabasca bituminous sands area, Alberta

Details: Project located at 15-88-8 W4 on Texaco's bituminous sands Lease No. 51.
                Applications for amendments to original approval has been approved. Project
                features a 27-hole program.

Project Cost: $3 million

Status: Active

* * *

Principal: Union Oil Company of Canada (87% owned by Union Oil Company of California)

Project
 Description: Experimental in situ recovery project west of Athabasca deposit, Alberta,
                Canada

Details: Union operated under Approval No. 2062 in 21-89-21 W4 in the Chipewyan area.
                Project involved a single well huff-andpuff test.

Status: Completed

* * *

Principal: Union Texas of Canada, Ltd.

Project
 Description: Experimental in situ recovery project in Cold Lake deposit, Alberta, Canada

Details: Project is located at 20-62-3 W4 in the Ardmore area on Lease No. 56 held by Union Texas. Production of 500 BPCD is expected from the 16 well formation using huff-and-puff recovery techniques. Authorized production is 1,000 BPCD.

Status: Active

* * *

Principal: World Wide Energy Company

Project
Description: Experimental in situ recovery project in Cold Lake deposit, Alberta, Canada

Details: World Wide Energy Co. is currently assessing the potential of deposits in the Fort Kent area of Alberta (Sec. 28, 761). Plans for Phase I of the project would entail drilling 14 wells on 160-acre spacing to gain reservoir information. At present, one well is being steamed. The huff-and-puff method is being used. World Wide gained ERCB approval 10/3/75. Production from the single well has now been achieved at 70 BPD after injection of 20,00 bbls. of steam. Well is producing no sand is pumping 15 percent water with the oil. Four more wells to be drilled in 1976.

Project Cost: Undetermined

Status: Production and expansion underway

* * *

SYNTHETIC FUELS FROM COAL

COMMERCIAL PROJECT

Principals: ANG Coal Gasification Co., and Michigan Wisconsin Pipeline Co. (wholly owned subsidiaries of American Natural Gas Co.)

Project Name: ANG Coal Gasification Project

Project
Description: Commercial plants - SNG from coal

Details: Overall plans call for four 250-MMCFD gasification plants in west central North Dakota. First plant planned for start-up in 1981; other plants scheduled at four-year intervals thereafter. North American Coal Corp. has dedicated a 3.7 billion ton lignite reserve to project. State has awarded a conditional water permit for 17,000 AFY from Lake Sakakawea to serve first plant. C. E. Lummus & Kaiser Engineers are committed to project thru first plant. Filed for first plant with FPC in March 1975.

Project Cost: Estimated in fall of 1975 constant dollars
             Plant - $943 million
             Mine - $168 million

Status: Pending FPC certification

* * *

Principal: Burlington Northern

Project Name: Circle West Project

Project
Description: Commercial plant - fertilizer and liquid products from coal.

Details: BN is studying the feasibility of a coal mine and conversion facility to be located on the Dreyer Bros. Ranch (subsidiary of BN) near Circle, in McCone County, Montana. Details concerning the type and size of facility have not been released. BN has filed with the State of Montana for 67,000 AFY of water from Fort Peck Reservoir.

Status: Planning

* * *

Principals: Cities Service Gas Co. & Northern Natural Gas Co.

Project
Description: Commercial plants - SNG from coal

Details: Joint pursuit of coal gasification in Powder River basin of Montana-Wyoming for gasification to 1,000 MMCFD SNG in four plants of 250 MMCFD capacity. The dedication of 500 million tons of coal by Peabody Coal Co. to the project is contingent on renegotiation of the lease contract with the Northern Cheyenne Indian Nation (Montana).

Status: Under study

* * *

Principal: Colorado Interstate Gas Co.

Project
Description: Commercial plant - SNG from coal

Details: CIG has a 10-year option on a large block of coal land in Montana from Westmoreland Resources. Estimated reserves are 300 million tons. CIG has helped to finance a pilot plant project by Occidental Petroleum's Garret Research. CIG's parent company, Coastal States Gas Corp., is conducting process and economic evaluations.

Status: No announcements since signing of the 10-year lease option, December 1971

* * *

Principal: Columbia Coal Gasification Corp.

Project
Description: Commercial plant - medium BTU gas from coal

Details: Columbia has completed preliminary studies for a facility to provide 700 MMSCFD of 300 BTU/CF gas for the Lukens Steel Co., Coastesville, Pa. It is proposed that the Koppers-Totzek coal gasification process be used. The construction schedule has not been announced.

Project Cost: Estimated at $114 million

Status: Active - pending financing plan

* * *

Principal: Consolidated Natural Gas Co.

Project
Description: Commercial plant - medium BTU gas from coal

Details: CNG has been conducting feasibility studies for a facility to produce between 230 and 330 MMSCFD of 300 BTU/CF gas from bituminous coal for industrial and utility use. The facility could be located in Ohio, West Virginia or Pennsylvania and may use Koppers-Totzek, Babcock and Wilcox or Texaco gasification processes.

Project Cost: Estiamted at $120 million

Status: Active

* * *

Principal: Consumers Power Co.

Project
Description: Commercial plant - medium BTU gas from coal

Details: Consumers Power proposes to construct a facility to produce 188 MM SCFD of 300 BTU/CF gas from bituminous coal for the Karn generating station (retrofit) Units 3 and 4, located at Bay City, Michigan. Riley Stoker and Koppers-Totzek gasification processes are being considered. Consumers that it will respond to ERDA's RFD for a low/medium - BTU coal gasification demonstration plant.

Project Cost: Estimated at $180 million

Status: Active

* * *

Principal: El Paso Natural Gas Co.

Project Name: Burnham Coal Gasification Project

Project
Description: Commercial plants - SNG from coal

Details: Initial capacity of complex will be 288 MMCFD with sufficient water and coal reserves to support ultimate total capacity of 785 MMCFD. Lurgi gasification technology will be used. Complex site is to be on a coal lease held jointly by El Paso and Consolidation Coal Company on the Navajo Indian Reservation in northwestern New Mexico. Application has been made to Bureau of Reclamation

for 28,250 AFY from the Navajo Reservoir. BuRec's Draft Environmental
Statement circulated July 1974. Final FPC rate decision has been deferred
at El Paso's request.

Project Cost: Estimated at $1 billion

Status: Pending FPC certification and consumation of coal and water contracts

* * *

Principal: El Paso Natural Gas Co.

Project
Description: Commercial plant - SNG from coal

Details: El Paso has announced intentions of building four plants in North Dakota.
Reserves of two billion tons are under lease in Bowman, Stark and Dunn
Counties. First plant scheduled on stream by 1981. El Paso recently with-
drew an application for 71,800 AFY from Lake Sakakawea filed with the N.D.
state water commission.

Status: Planning

* * *

Principal: Exxon Corp. (Carter Oil)

Project
Description: Commercial plant - SNG from coal

Details: Carter Oil, a subsidiary of Exxon Corp., is studying the possibility of
constructing a coal gasification plant in northern Wyoming. Carter has
State and Federal leases in both Sheridan and Campbell counties; however,
the probable location of the plant will be near Gillette, Wyo., in Campbell
County. Also, Carter has an industrial water contract for 50,000 AFY from
the Yellowtail Unit on the Big Horn River.

Project Cost: Project cost - $400-500 million for commercial plant

Status: Planning

* * *

Principals: Illinois Coal Gasification Group - 8 Companies

.Project
Description: Commercial plant - SNG from coal

Details: The group consisting of Central Illinois Light Co., Central Illinois Public
Service, Commonwealth Edison Co., Illinois Power Co., Iowa Illinois Gas and
Electric Co., Northern Illinois Gas Co., Peoples Gas Light and Coke Co.,
and North Shore Gas Co., seeks to construct a coal gasification facility in
Illinois. In January 1976, the group responded to ERDA's RFP for a high BTU
coal gasification demonstration plant.

Status: Investigating feasibility

* * *

Principal: Louisiana Municipal Power Commission (LAMPCO)

Project
Description: Commercial plan - low BTU gas from coal

Details: LAMPCO'proposes to construct a facility at Baldwin, Louisiana, to produce
78 MM SCFD of 140 BTU/CF gas (115 MW) from bituminous coal and residual oil
for power generation. Economic and engineering studies incorporating the Texaco
coal gasification process have been completed.

Project Cost: Estimated at $62 million

Status: Active

* * *

Principals: Natural Gas Pipeline Company of America a wholly-owned subsidiary of the
Peoples Gas Company

Project Name: Dunn Center Coal Gasification Project

Project
Description: Commercial plants - SNG from coal

Details: NGPL has received rights to 2.1 billion tons of lignite from the Nokota
Company under a 20-year lease agreement, Jan. '73, covering 110,000 acres
in Central Dunn County, North Dakota. NGPL has applied to the North Dakota
Water Commission for eventual use of 70,000 AFY of water for both mining
and gasification. First of four planned 250 MMCFD Lurgi plants is currently
envisioned to be operating by 1952 with successive plants following at three-
year intervals. Fluor will be the engineering contractor for the project.
Dames and Moore will be conducting environmental work also. FPC filing is
planned for early 1976.

Project Cost: Estimated at $1 billion

Status: Planning studies underway

* * *

Principals: Panhandle Eastern Pipeline Co. and Peabody Coal Co.

Project
Description: Commercial plant - SNG from coal

Details: Capacity is 270 MMCFD.Lurgi gasification methanation processes will be used.
The plant will be located about 15 miles northeast of Douglas, Wyoming.
Peabody has dedicated over 500 MM tons of coal tothe project, from a reserve
located in Campbell County. Coal will be delivered to the plant site by
railroad. Plant start-up is now predicted for the 1980-81 period, at the
earliest. Bechtel and SERNCO are the general and environmental contractors,
respectively, SASOL has been retained as a consultant. The state has issued a
1974 appropriation to take water from the North Platte and permit to construct
a 26,000 acre-foot surface reservoir. Up to 5,000 AFY is appro ved from the
existing LaPrele Reservoir which is to be rehabilitated by Panhandle.

Project Cost: Estimated at $1 billion

Status: Design and development is proceeding

* * *

Principal: South African Coal, Oil and Gas Corporation Limited (Sasol)

Project Name: Sasol II

Project
Description: Sasol II is a commercial project for the manufacture of synthetic motor
fuels using the Synthol (Fischer-Tropsch) process and employing coal as
basic raw material.

Details: Sasol II will be built on the eastern highveld of Transvaal. Estimated
coal (low grade) consumption is 12 million ton per annum. The facilities
comprise the following plants:

   Boiler house
   Lurgi gasification
   Oxygen
   Rectisol gas purification, gasification by-products recovery,
   Synthol
   Refinery, and gas reforming

Plant capacity is 1.75 million ton per annum of Fischer-Tropsch products,
287,000 tpa tar products, 100,000 tpa ammonia and 75,000 tpa sulfur

Over-all contractor is Fluor Engineers and Constructors, Inc. of Los Angeles

Completion date expected to be March 1981

Project Cost: Estimated mid-1974 at $1.4 billion

Status: Project approved in December 1974. Over-all contractors appointed in
March 1975. Process and detailed design in progress.

* * *

Principal: Texaco, Inc.

Project
Description: Commercial plant - SNG or liquid products from coal

Details: Texaco acquired, Oct. '73, rights to coal reserves estimated at 2 billion
              tons and certain water rights from Reynolds Metals Co. These reserves are
              located near Lake DeSmet in Wyoming on some 37,000 acres. Commercial plant
              employing either a gasification or liquefaction process could result. Green
              Construction Co. of Des Moines, Iowa has started on a multi-million-dollar
              water development system. Completion is expected in 1976. Morrison-Knudsen
              Co. will do an engineering study of Texaco's coal, land, and water holding.
              Texaco announced, June 1975, that it has contracted with Genge Resources, Inc.
              for collection of baseline environmental data and the preparation of an En-
              vironmental Impact Assessment. In January, 1976, Texaco, Inc., Natural Gas
              Pipeline Co. of America, Peoples Gas Co., Montana-Dakota Utilities Co. and
              Pacific Gas and Electric Co., through the joint venture Company - WYCOALGAS
              Group, responded to ERDA's RFP for a high-BTU coal gasification plant, pro-
              posing the facility be constructed near Texaco's Lake DeSmet holdings.

Status: Planning studies and water development work underway

                                  * * *

Principals: Texas Eastern Transmission Corp. & Pacific Lighting Corp. formed Western
              Gasification Co. (WESCO) to own and operate plant

Project Name: WESCO Coal Gasification Project

Project
Description: Commercial plants - SNG from coal

Details: Lurgi gasifiers will produce 250 MMCFD of pipeline quality gas; possible
              expansion to 1,000 MMCFD. Plant will be located adjacent to coal reserves
              held by Utah International Inc., on the Navajo Indian Reservation in north-
              western, N.M. Fluor Corp., did feasibility study and Battelle prepared the
              environmental impact statement. Approximately 9.6 million tons of coal per
              year, along with sufficient water rights to operate the plant will be pur-
              chased from Utah International under terms of a 25-year contract. Gas will
              be sold to the Pacific Lighting Service Corp. (75%) and Cities Service Gas
              Co. (25%). Construction and mining permits granted by the New Mexico Air
              Quality Division on September 27, 1974, and the New Mexico Surfacemining
              Commission on July 25, 1974, respectively. FPC final decision (opinion
              No. 728) rendered 4/21/75, amended 11/21/75 after rehearing (Docket
              No. CP73-211). Final EIS issued by Bureau of Reclamation 1/14/76.

Project Cost: $852.9 million

Status: Pending FPC certification

                                  * * *

Principals: Texas Gas Transmission Corp. and State of Kentucky

Project
Description: Commercial plant - SNG from coal

Details: Texas Gas has acquired from Consolidation Coal Co., a half interest in an
              extensive block of coal reserves in the Illinois Basin area. The reserves
              are in two parcels. Approximately 3.5 trillion SCF of SNG are recoverable
              from the reserve. Texas Gas and the State of Kentucky, through a joint
              venture, Ken-Tex Energy Corp. propose a two phase program to develop a coal
              gasification complex to be located on the Ohio river in Western Kentucky:
              Phase one - 80 MM SCFD demonstration plant by 1980; Phase two - 250 MM
              SCFD commercial facility by 1983. Ken-Tex, in response (January, 1976) to
              ERDA's RFP for a high-BTU coal gasification demonstration plant, proposed a
              $400 million facility utilizing the HYGAS process.

Status: Planning studies underway

                                  * * *

Principal: TransCanada Pipelines, Ltd.

Project
Description: Commercial plant - SNG from coal

Details: TransCanada has initiated a study to determine the feasibility of constructing
              a 250-MMCFD coal gasification plant in western Canada using Lurgi technology.
              Plant location is to be based on evaluation by Lurgi or representative samples
              from as many as four west Canadian coal fields. TransCanada has been un-
              successful in obtaining NEB approval for inclusion of $8 million in rate base -
              resubmission of application is expected.

Project Cost: $8 million for feasibility study and down payment of critical capital equipment

Status: Proposed

* * *

Principal: <u>UGI, Corp.</u>

Project
Description: <u>Commercial plant - Methanol from coal derived synthesis gas</u>

Details: <u>UGI is planning to construct in Pennsylvania or Ohio a facility using the
              Texaco coal gasification process to produce 2500 tpd of methanol from
              5000 tpd of bituminous coal. The methanol is anticipated to be marketed as
              a utility/industrial fuel or as a chemical feedstock.</u>

Project Cost: <u>Estimated at $300 million</u>

Status: <u>Active</u>

* * *

DEMONSTRATION, PILOT OR RESEARCH PROJECTS

Principals: COGAS Development Company (CDC), joint venture of Consolidated Natural Gas,
              FMC Corp., Panhandle Eastern Pipeline, and Tennessee Gas Pipeline

Project
Description: Pilot plant - SNG and synthetic crude oil from coal at Leatherhead, England

Details: Pilot plant facility in Leatherhead has achieved several successful test
              runs and is in the final stages of feasibility testing. The plant has a
              feed capacity equivalent to 100 tons of coal per day, and is operated
              under contract with the British Coal Utilization Research Association.
              Future runs are anticipated to be of longer duration and intended to opti-
              mize process variables. CDC is also continuing with the assistance of
              Bechtel, Inc. to evaluate comparative process alternatives and conduct
              preliminary economic and technical evaluations for a larger scale operation.

Project Cost: Initial development program, including pilot plants, estimated at $8.5 million.

Status: Operational

* * *

Principals: Commonwealth Edison Co., EPRI, and Fluor Corp. - sponsors

Project
Description: Demonstration plant - gasification turbine test facility

Details: Commonwealth is helping to finance, with assistance from Electric Power
              Research Institute, build and operate a plant near Pekin, Illinois close
              to its existing power plant. Lurgi gasifier will be used to process 60 T/hr
              of coal and produce 120 BTU/CF gas for a 25,000 KW generation unit. A test
              facility with commercial size equipment will allow Edison to scale-up the
              process to a 500 MW unit. Fluor Corp. has been named contractor for the
              operation.

Project Cost: Undetermined

Status: Active

* * *

Principal: Conoco Methanation Co., (subsidiary of Continental Oil Co.)

Project
Description: Demonstration plant - methanation of coal gas

Details: Plant was adjacent to and methanated purified gas from the Scottish Gas
              Board's Lurgi gasifiers at Westfield, Scotland. Conoco designed the
              facilities; Woodall-Duckham constructed the plant. British Gas Council
              acted as consultant. 13 companies participated with Conoco. Plant
              operated successfully producing high methane gas (95%) at rates of 2.5 MMCFD.

Project Cost: Estimated at $6 million
Status: Methanation tests completed

* * *

Principals: Continental Oil Co., and 13 other U.S. companies

Project
Description: Demonstration plant - coal gasification

Details: The three-year test program will involve the modification of a Lurgi gasifier
              at the Westfield, Scotland gas plant for operation under slagging conditions.
              Conoco will coordinate project and British Gas Corp. will be project operator.
              This slagging process was tested on a pilot plant scale during the 1962-64
              period by BGC. Advantages claimed for this modification are lower steam
              consumption, higher throughput and higher thermal efficiency.

Project Cost: Estimated at $10 million
Status: Operational

* * *

Principals: Electric Power Research Institute and the Southern Services Co. - sponsor,
              Catalytic, Inc. - contractor

Project
Description: Pilot plant - solvent refining of coal

Details: Plant is on the site of Southern Electric Generating Company's E. C. Gaston
              Steam Plant near Wilsonville, Alabama. It was designed, built and is operated
              by Catalytic, Inc. The process dissolves coal under pressure in the presence
              of a small quantity of hydrogen. Through the use of filters and other sepa-
              ration processes, ash content is reduced to about 0.1 percent; sulfur content
              can be reduced to as low as 0.3 percent. Plant capacity is 6 TPD. The product
              is a clean fuel containing approximately 90 percent of the carbon in the ori-
              ginal coal. A 75 day continuous run has been completed.

Project Cost: Total 1975 cost to construct and operate the plant was $11.3 million with
              EPRI contributing $7.8 million, Southern Services $3.5 million.

Status: Operational

* * *

Principals: EPRI - sponsor, B&W - contractor

Project
Description: Design study - coal gasification

Details: EPRI is funding detailed design studies for a 20 tons/hour entrained bed
              gasification unit by Babcock & Wilcox to operate at 50 psig.

Project Cost: Undetermined
Status: B&W submitting proposal to ERDA for additional funding

* * *

Principals: EPRI - sponsor, Combustion Engineering - contractor

Project
Description: Design study - coal gasification

Details: EPRI is funding detailed design studies by Combustion Engineering for a
              5 tons/hour atmospheric pressure coal gasification unit.

Project Cost: Undetermined
Status: Combustion Engineering recently obtained partial funding for this project
              from ERDA. Additional funding from ERDA will be sought.

* * *

Principal: El Paso Natural Gas Co.

Project Name: Development Coal Gasifier Project.

Project
Description: Pilot plant - SNG from coal.

Details: One Lurgi module located at Burnham, New Mexico for process development
              to test: capacity, low BTU production, gasification of coal fines, various

coals and environmental aspects. Land reclamation will proceed concurrently. FPC has granted intermediate approval for inclusion of development costs in rate base.

Project Cost: Undetermined

Status: Pending final FPC decision in commercial project rate case

* * *

Principals: ERDA/Fossil Energy and American Gas Association

Project Name: Lurgi Process Development

Project
Description: Pilot plant - SNG from coal

Details: Modification of the Lurgi reactor to permit handling of coking and swelling American coals. Tests were made in Scottish Gas Board's Lurgi plant at Westfield, Scotland. Lurgi was responsible for internal reactor modification while Woodall-Duckham made necessary ancillary system modification to isolate the single gasifier unit. Technological guidance was provided by the the British Gas Corp. and Lurgi throughout the program. Some 20,000 tons of the following U.S. coals were tested: Illinois No. 5, Illinois No. 6, Pittsburgh No. 8, and Montana Rosebud.

Project Cost: Undetermined

Status: Tests completed - final report has been published

* * *

Principals: ERDA/Fossil Energy and American Gas Association - Sponsor Battelle Columbus - contractor.

Project Name: Agglomerating Burner Project

Project
Description: Pilot plant - SNG from coal

Details: A 25-TPD pilot plant is being built by Chemico at Battelle's West Jefferson, Ohio Laboratories to investigate the Agglomerating Burner Process proposed and developed by Battelle under sponsorship of Union Carbide Corporation.

Project Cost: $8.85 million

Status: Construction in progress

* * *

Principals: ERDA/Fossil Energy and American Gas Association - sponsors, Bituminous Coal Research, Inc. - Contractor, Phillips Petroleum - Operator

Project Name: BI-GAS·Project

Project
Description: Pilot plant - SNG from coal

Details: The entrained bed process, developed by Bituminous Coal Research, Inc., reacts pulverized coal in a stream of oxygen and steam at high temperature and pressure to produce SNG. Stearns-Roger Corp. to design and build the pilot plant to process five TPH to produce 100 MCFH of pipeline gas. Plant site is Homer City, Pennsylvania.

Project Cost: Estimated at $30 million

Status: Testing to begin in early 1976

* * *

Principals: ERDA/Fossil Energy, American Gas Association - sponsors, Chem Systems - contractor

Project
Description: Process development unit - liquid phase methanation (LPM).

Details: A skid mounted LPM pilot unit constructed by Davy Powergas is to be installed at either the HYGAS or CO_2-Acceptor coal gasification pilot plants for evaluation by the second quarter of 1976. The unit has a capicity of 2MMSCFD of synthesis gas feed.

Project Cost: Current contract - $2.2 million

Status: Pilot unit construction near completion

* * *

Principals: ERDA/Fossil Energy, American Gas Association - sponsors, Consolidation Coal
                  Co. - contractor

Project Name: CO_2 Acceptor Project

Project
Description: Pilot plant - SNG from coal

Details: Plant located at Rapid City, South Dakota is designed to produce 2 MMCFD of
                  375 BUT/SCF gas from 40 tons of lignite and 3 tons of dolomite per day. In
                  the CO_2 Acceptor process developed by Consol, ground lignite is fed into the
                  gasifier under pressure of 150 to 300 psi and heated to 1,560°F   by steam.
                  Dolomite, preheated to 1,900°F   is introduced into the gasifier to chemically
                  remove free CO_2 from the produced gas stream by the exothermic CO_2 Acceptor
                  reaction. Gas purification and packed tube methanation units to start-up
                  soon.

Project Cost: $9.3 million for construction and an estimated $5 million annually for oper-
                  ation

Status: Operational

* * *

Principals: ERDA/Fossil Energy, American Gas Association - sponsors, Institute of Gas
                  Technology - contractor

Project Name: HYGAS Project

Project
Description: Pilot plant - SNG from coal

Details: Pilot plant capacity is 1.5 MMSCFD of SNG. The process involves the simul-
                  taneous reaction of coal with process derived hydrogen and steam. Alternative
                  processes under development for hydrogen production are: electrothermal,
                  steam-oxygen and steam-iron. ERDA reported that in a test run in July '75
                  steady state conditions were achieved for 160 hours. The plant is now in
                  operation with Illinois No. 6 bituminous coal.

Project Cost: total ERDA/AGA commitment since 1964 has been $55.1 million; steam oxygen
                  development program, $16.5 million; steam-iron development program, $18.2 million

Status: Operational

* * *

Principals: ERDA/Fossil Energy - sponsor, Bituminous Coal Research - contractor

Project
Descripiton: Process development unit - low-BTU gas from coal

Details: PDU to develop fluid bed low-BTU coal gasification

Project Cost: $2.5 million (estimated)

Status: Unit shakedown underway

* * *

Principals: ERDA/Fossil Energy, Sun, ARCO, Ashland, Mobil, Dupont, Reynolds, Martin Marietta,
              Consolidated Gas, Y and O Coal, and EPRI - sponsors, Coalcon - contractors

Project Name: Coalcon Clean Boil Fuels from Coal Project

Project
Description: Demonstration Plant - SNG and liquid products from coal

Details: Coalcon will design, construct and operate a 2,600 TPD demonstration plant us-
              ing a hydrocarbonization process for producing 3,900 barrels/day of 17°API
              liquid product and 22 MMCFD of SNG. The project is framed in four phases over
              eight years. The Coalcon Plant is to be located near New Athens,
              Illinois on a 2,000 acre site, much of which has previously been strip mined
              for coal. Coalcon is a joint venture of Union Carbide and Chemical Construc-
              tion Corporation.

Project Cost: Estimated at $256 million

Status: Plant design and procurement underway

* * *

Principals: ERDA/Fossil Energy - sponsor, Combustion Engineering - contractor

Project
Description: Process development unit - low-BTU gas from coal

Details: Four-year, three-phase program to demonstrate the C-E atmospheric entrainment gasification system to produce low-BTU gas. A 5 TPH PDU will be designed, constructed and operated by C-E at C-E's Windsor, Connecticut site. Determination of investment and operating costs for a commercial scale plant will follow under the final project phase.

Project Cost: $20.6 million.

Status: Pilot plant design under way

* * *

Principals: ERDA/Fossil Energy, Consolidation Coal Co. and Continental Oil Co. - sponsors, Morgantown Energy   Research Center - contractor

Project
Description: Underground coal gasification project

Details: The project is designed to assess the potential value of coal gasification in thin eastern coal beds. Project site will be Grants District of Wetzel County, West Virginia. The process will use directional drilling techniques to place parallel, horizontal, holes through the coal bed. Air will be injected to sustain gasification and partial combustion. The process will rely on natural porosity of the bed for product gas accumulation. The 5-phase project will cover preparation, field testing, and technical, environmental and social evaluation.

Project Cost: $10 million for the five-year project.

Status: Active with field work underway

* * *

Principals: ERDA/Fossil Energy, Shell Development Corp. - sponsors, Continental Oil Co. - contractor

Project
Description: Bench scale - liquid products from coal

Details: Conoco Coal Development Division at Library, Pennsylvania is to test the potential application of a zinc-halide hydrocracking process to produce distillate fuel from coal. Four barrels per ton is expected. A 100 pound per hour test unit is under development.

Project Cost: Estimated at $6.5 million

Status: Testing is underway

* * *

Principals: ERDA/Fossil Energy - sponsor, Eyring Research Institute - contractor

Project
Description: Bench scale - low-BTU gas from coal

Details: Research is aimed at development of a high specific rate gasifier to produce gas of about 300 BTU/SCF at a 70 percent or greater thermal efficiency. A bench scale gasifier operating at 50-100 lbs of coal/hr has shown consistent results and reasonably high efficiency.

Project Cost: Undertermined

Status: Studies in progress

* * *

Principals: ERDA/Fossil Energy - Sponsor, Fluor Corp. - Contractor

Project
Description: Pilot plant - liquid products from coal

Details: Fluor Engineers and Constructors has a contract to convert the former coal-to-gasoline pilot plant in Cresap, West Virginia to a multiprocess test facility for coal liquefaction processes. The former program was terminated in 1970. In addition to procurement and construction services, Fluor will manage the overall program.

Project Cost: $13 million for 3-year contract

Status: Construction underway

* * *

Principals: ERDA/Fossil Energy - Sponsor, FMC Corp. - Contractor

Project Name: COED Project

Project
Description: Pilot plant - liquid products from coal

Details: Pilot plant at Princeton, N. J. had a capacity of 36 TPD yielding 30 BPD of
             refinery feedstock plus char and fuel gas. Plant has operated on seven coals
             from west, midwest and eastern fields. Char was tested in July 1975 in a
             commercial Koppers-Totzek gasifier in Spain with report to be issued in early
             1976 Pilot plant data deemed to be complete and operations have been dis-
             continued.

Project Cost: Over $20 million

Status: Completed - final report to be issued in early 1976

* * *

Principals: ERDA/Fossil Energy - Sponsor, Foster-Wheeler and Bethlehem Steel Co. -
             Contractors

Project Name Synthoil Project

Project
Description: Process Development Unit - liquid products from coal

Details: Foster Wheeler is to design a 10 TPD coal liquefaction PDU using the
             Synthoil process. The coal is converted catalytically slurried with process
             derived oil, to produce synthetic crude. The scaled-up plant will be located
             at Bruceton, Pennsylvania and will be constructed and operated by Bethlehem
             Steel Co. Start-up is expected in 1976. A 500 TPD pilot plant is proposed.

Project Cost: $6.9 million (present contract value)

Status: Design of PDU underway

* * *

Principals: ERDA/Fossil Energy, Foster-Wheeler, <u>Northern States Power Co., and Empire
             State Electric Energy Research Corp.</u> - Sponsors, Foster Wheeler - Contractor

Project
Description: Pilot Plant - low-BTU gas from coal for combined cycle power generation

Details: Foster-Wheeler is to design and prepare construction bids for a low-BTU coal
             gasification pilot plant under phase two of the four phase program. Phases
             three and four will include construction and operation. <u>The pilot unit, to
             be constructed at Northern States Lawrence Station, Sioux Falls, South Dakota,
             is to use an air blown version of the BI-GAS coal gasifier. The unit is to
             produce 125-150 BTU/CF gas to fire a 34 MW combined cycle power generating
             unit</u>.

Project Cost: <u>ERDA - $60 million</u>
             <u>Industry - $30 million</u>

Status: Pilot plant design has begun

* * *

Principals: ERDA/Fossil Energy,Sun, Ashland, Shell, Standard of Indiana, Commonwealth of
             Kentucky, and EPRI - Sponsors, Hydrocarbon Research, Inc. - Contractor

Project Name: H-Coal Project

Project
Description: Pilot plant - low-sulfur fuel oil and other liquid products from coal.

Details: 600 TPD pilot plant to test the commercial potential of H-Coal liquefaction
             process is to be built at Catlettsburg, Kentucky. The plant design calls for
             the production of 0.7 percent fuel oil from 3.0 percent coal. The three-phase
             project will cover plant design, construction, and operation, respectively.
             Under phase one HRI is completing testing at Trenton, New Jersey and gathering
             data for environmental, technical, and economic assessment. Fluor Engineers
             and Constructors has been selected as design contractor. <u>ARCO has dropped
             out of the H-Coal Project</u>.

Project Cost: $8.1 million for phase one

Status: Pilot plant in design stage

* * *

Principals: ERDA/Fossil Energy - Sponsor, Laramie Energy Research Center - Contractor

Project Name: Hanna Project

Project
Description: Underground coal gasification

Details: The linked vertical well process being developed at Hanna, Wyoming is in the
              second phase of experimentation (air blown) and is directed at the gasification
              of coal seams between 15 and 50 feet thick. This involves the linkage of well
              bores by reverse combustion followed by gasification by forward combustion. A
              seam weep test is planned for early 1976.

Project Cost: Undetermined

Status: Field Experiments underway

* * *

Principals: ERDA/Fossil Energy - Sponsor, Lawrence Livermore Laboratory - Contractor

Project
Description: Underground coal gasification

Details: The LLL packed bed process is being developed for the gasification of coal seams
              greater than 50 ft. thick and at depths greater than 500 ft. Chemical explos-
              ives are used to fracture the reaction zone. Gas collection is from the bottom
              of the reaction zone with oxygen/steam injected towards the top to sustain com-
              bustion and gasification. Field work for the first experiment has begun at a
              site on Hoe Creek, 25 miles southwest of Gillette, Wyoming.

Project Cost: ERDA funding at $3.3 million for FY '75.

Status: Field work underway

* * *

Principals: ERDA/Fossil Energy - Sponsor, A. D. Little, Inc. - Contractor

Project
Description: Bench scale - liquid products from coal

Details: Project consists of an exploratory experimental program at the bench scale with
              a 20 to 40 lb. extractive coker at Foster-Wheeler. Data will be provided for
              design of a pilot plant. Work is to be conducted in conjunction with an ex-
              perimental laboratory investigation at the Pittsburgh Energy Research Center
              at Bruceton, Pennsylvania.

Project Cost: $0.57 million

Status: Study in progress

* * *

Principals: ERDA/Fossil Energy - Sponsor, University of North Dakota Engineering Experi-
              ment Station - Contractor

Project
Description: Process Development Unit - SNG and liquid products from lignite

Details: A process development unit of approximately 50 lb/hr capacity will be used for
              the solvent refining of lignite. Data generated in autoclave experiments and
              bench-scale tests are being used to design the PDU.

Project Cost: $3.4 million (five year contract)

Status: PDU tests underway

* * *

Principals: ERDA/Fossil Energy - Sponsor, Oak Ridge National Laboratory - Contractor

Project
Description: Bench scale - SNG from coal

Details: ORNL is conducting hydrogasification bench scale studies with a continuous
              10 lb/hr fluid bed reactor to determine optimum reactor design and reaction
              conditions. Other projects include: catalyst development, petrographic
              studies, and laboratory support to Lawrence Livermore Laboratory's under-
              ground coal gasification project.

Project Cost: Undetermined

Status: Active

* * *

Principals: ERDA/Fossil Energy - Sponsor, Pittsburg & Midway Coal Mining Co. - Contractor

Project Name: Solvent Refined Coal Project

Project
Description: Pilot plant - liquid products from coal

Details: The 50 TPD SRC pilot plant is located at Ft. Lewis, Washington. The plant
                produces 30 TPD of solvent refined coal (demineralized/low sulfur extract).
                The process has been developed by P&M from bench scale. The pilot plant was
                designed and constructed by Stearns-Roger and Rust Engineering, respectively.

Project Cost: $28 million contract to continue until 1976.

Status: Operational

* * *

Principals: ERDA/Fossil Energy - Sponsor, Ralph M. Parsons - Contractor

Project
Description: Process design and evaluation

Details: Parsons is to complete conceptual design for a commercial scale COED plant;
                evaluate the demonstration plant design for the solvent refined coal process;
                prepare preliminary commercial design for a Fischer-Tropsch conversion plant;
                prepare preliminary design for a complex to demonstrate various coal conver-
                sion processes beyond the pilot stage and preliminary design for a commercial
                SRC plant.

Project Cost: $3 million

Status: Studies in progress

* * *

Principals: ERDA/Fossil Energy - Sponsor, Pittsburgh Energy Research Center - Contractor

Project Name: Synthane Project

Project
Description: Pilot plant - SNG from coal

Details: This process, developed by the Bureau of Mines uses a steam-oxygen, fluid-bed
                gasifier to produce a pipeline-quality gas from coal. Pilot plant (72 T/D)
                is being started up, at Bruceton, Pennsylvania. Plant includes gas purific-
                ation and methanation units.

Project Cost: Undertermined

Status: Operational

* * *

Principals: ERDA/Fossil Energy - Sponsor, Rockwell International Corp., Northeast Utilities
                Service Co. - Contractor

Project
Description: Pilot plant - low-BTU gas from coal

Details: Rockwell to design, build and operate a 5 TPH plant to test molten sodium car-
                bonate process for low-BTU gas production for power generation. The system will
                operate at 1800°F and 10 atm. and will include salt regeneration and sulfur
                recovery units. The pilot plant will be located at Connecticut Light and Pow-
                er Company's Norwalk Harbor Generating Station. Forty-month program to obtain
                scale-up data and investigate air pollution emission control characteristics.

Project Cost: $6.9 million

Status: Plant design underway

* * *

Principals: ERDA/Fossil Energy - Sponsor, Rockwell International Corp. Rocketdyne Division
                - Contractor

Project
Description: Design and evaluation study - liquid products from coal

Details: Rockwell International Corp. to develop coal liquefaction process by direct
                hydrogenation using the Rocketdyne process. Technique involves mixing and
                conditioning of two streams, coal and hydrogen, almost instantaneously. Con-
                version process forms light hydrocarbon liquids and gases and prevents break-
                down of larger, complex molecules. Project to consist of low flow testing
                followed by design and fabrication of large-scale reactor for demonstration
                purposes. Rocketdyne process originally developed for propellant injection
                in liquid fuel rocket engines.

Project Cost: $1 million

Status: Studies in progress

* * *

Principals: ERDA/Fossil Energy - Sponsor, University of Utah - Contractor

Project
Description: Bench scale - process evaluation, SNG and liquid products from coal

Details: The University of Utah under a four-year contract will conduct process eval-
              uations, catalytic liquefaction studies, and evaluation of coal conversion
              products.

Project Cost: $2.6 million

Status: Active

* * *

Principals: ERDA/Fossil Energy, Public Service Indiana, Bechtel Corp., AMAX Coal Co. and
              Peabody Coal Co. - Sponsors, Westinghouse Electric Corp. - Contractor

Project
Description: Process development plant - low-BTU gas from coal

Details: The project will involve a six-phase development. First is a 1200 lb/hr pro-
              cess development plant supported by laboratory investigations to confirm oper-
              ational data received from the PDU. This will be followed by building and
              operating a five-ton/hr pilot plant. A 50 ton/hr power plant will then be
              built and operated by Public Service Indiana at their Dresser facility. The
              process will provide a clean burning gas with a heating value of 120 to 160
              BTU/SCF.

Project Cost: Total program cost estimated at $80 million; Westinghouse has an $8.2 million
              contract from ERDA for 70 percent of the initial R&D cost.

Status: PDU tests active

* * *

Principal: Exxon Corporation

Project
Description: Pilot plant - liquid products from coal

Details: A two-phase program is underway to develop a coal liquefaction process with
              the first phase being design and the second being construction and operation
              of a 250 TPD pilot plant. A companion project by Exxon to develop a coal gas-
              ification process was postponed in November 1974.

Project Cost: Project cost - Phase one - $10 million, Phase two - $145 million

Status: Active

* * *

Principals: General Electric Company - Sponsor and Investigator (Gasifier), Electric
              Power Research Inst. - Sponsor (Operation and Extrusion R&D)

Project Name: GEGAS-D Project

Project
Description: Pilot Plant, Low-BTU gas from coal

Details: The construction and erection of a one TPH, 23 atmosphere fixed bed gas pro-
              ducer is underway in Schenectady. Checkout runs began Feb. '76. The unit
              is equipped to study gasification of highly caking fuels at reduced steam/air
              ratios under clinkering conditions. Test results on a wide range of coals in
              a 50 pound per hour atmospheric gasifier provided many of the design bases.
              Coal extrusion feeding and tar balances are to be developed on GEGAS-D. Plans
              are underway to ultimately have this facility supply gas to gas cleaning,
              and gas combustion apparatus. The goal is to provide design bases for
              an integrated coal-fired gas turbine combined cycle.

Project Cost: Undertermined

Status: Operational

* * *

Principal: Gulf Research and Development

Project Name: Catalytic Coal Liquefaction Project

Project
Description: Pilot plant - liquid products from coal

Details: In the CCL Process slurried coal plus hydrogen at 2,000-4,000 psi passes over a catalyst to yield two to four barrels of low sulfur liquid fuel per ton, depending on type of coal charged. The process is capable of converting lignite, subbituminous or bituminous coal. Three pilot project plants are currently in operation, the largest of which has a capacity of 1 TPD of coal.

Project Cost: Undertermined

Status: Operational

* * *

Principals: Institute of Gas Technology and Ralph M. Parsons Co.

Project Name: U-Gas Project

Project
Description: Pilot plant - low-BTU gas from coal

Details: Parsons will engineer and design a demonstration gasifier to fuel a 50-100 MW power generation plant. Industry and government financing is being sought. Process reacts crushed coal with air and steam in a single-stage fluidized-bed gasifier at pressure of about 300 psig. Produced gas has a heating value of 140 BTU/SCF. Sulfur and particulates are removed from the raw gas in a high temperature cleanup system. Plant site not yet selected.

Project Cost: Undetermined

Status: Active

* * *

Principals: Island Creek Coal Co. and Garrett Laboratories (both subsidiaries of Occidental Petroleum)

Project
Description: Pilot plant - liquid products from coal

Details: Planning is underway for a 200 TPD pilot plant to convert coal to fuel oil using Garrett's pyrolysis process developed to produce fuel oil from municipal solid waste. Sponsors are being sought for a four year program.

Project Cost: $6 million

Status: Active

* * *

Principals: Stone & Webster Engineering Corp. and General Atomic Co.

Project
Description: Process evaluation

Details: Joint program to use GA's HTGC nuclear reactor to provide heat for S&W's solution-hydrogasification coal conversion process. Two-year R & D program to be managed by S&W. Industry support being sought.

Project Cost: First phase estimated at $650,000 (San Diego Gas & Electric has committed $100,000).

Status: Active

* * *

Principals: Swindell-Dressler Co. - Sponsor, Technology Application Service Corp. - Contractor

Project
Description: Process development unit - medium BTU gas from coal

Details: Swindell-Dressler Co., with Technology Application Service Corp., is working on a program to develop the Plasma Arc Torch Process on a subcommercial scale. Process would involve passing coal in a gas such as argon or hydrogen, in an anarobic environment, through an electric arc, which would generate a plasma flame 15,000°F-100,000°F, instantaneously gasifying the coal. High quality product gas would be methanated to achieve pipeline quality. Swindell-Dressler Co. is contacting several electric and gas utility companies about development of the project.

Project Cost: Undetermined

Status: Under development

* * *

Principal: Texas Utilities Services, Inc.

Project
Description: Underground gasification of Texas lignite

Details: Texas Utilities Services Inc., an affiliate of Dallas Power and Light Company,
                Texas Electric Service Company and Texas Power and Light Company, has purchased
                (through the Resource Sciences Corp., Tulsa, Oklahoma) underground gasification
                technology developed in the Soviet Union to determine the feasibility of gas-
                ifying deep lignite deposits in east Texas. A pilot plant is scheduled for
                operation in 1976 for gasification of lignite below 150 feet.

Project Cost: $2 million (process licensing)

Status: Active

* * *

Principal: United States Steel Corp.

Project Name: Clean Coke Project

Project
Description: Process development unit - liquid, gas and coke products from coal

Details: USS is currently operating a one quarter ton per day PDU to develop the Clean
                Coke process; using a combination of low-temperature carbonization and hy-
                drogenation to produce metallurgical coke, and low-sulfur liquid/gaseous
                fuels and chemical feed stocks. Design criteria are being developed for a
                4 TPD pilot plant. USS has reported: A Clean Coke plant processing 6.5
                million TPY of coal could yield 2.2 million tons of coke, 1.2 million tons
                of chemicals, 6 trillion BTUs in fuel gas and 670 thousand tons of coal residue
                from the hydrogenation process.

Project Cost: Undetermined

Status: PDU in operation

* * *

Principal: Universal Oil Products

Project
Description: Pilot plant - liquid products from coal

Details: High temperature and pressure hydrosolvation process producing four barrels
                of low-ash/low-sulfur syncrude per ton. Des Plaines, Illinois pilot plant
                to be enlarged.

Project Cost: Undetermined

Status: Active

* * *

Principals: University of Texas at Austin, National Science Foundation, Texas Utilities
                Service Company, Continental Oil Company, Mobile Oil Corporation, Shell Develop-
                ment Company, and Dow Chemical Company.

Project
Description: Underground gasification of Texas lignite

Details: Laboratory and limited field program to recover energy from lignite below
                stripping depth. Laboratory program focusing on chemical and physical prop-
                erties of lignite and overburden, subsidence, environmental effects, heat
                transfer, utilization of low-BTU gas, and lignite geology and hydrogeology.
                One year preliminary study indicated technical and economic feasibility and
                percolation method appears to be the most favorable approach. Process design
                for field test to be completed in 1977.

Project Cost: Undetermined

Status: Active

* * *

Principal: Wheelabrator-Frye, Inc.

Project
Description: Demonstration plant - solvent refined coal

Details: Wheelabrator-Frye is studying the feasibility of a 1,000 TPD plant to produce low sulfur/low ash coal using Gulf Oil's SRC process. The plant will provide fuel for power generation in Southern Company's system. The plant may be scaled to commercial capacity.

Project Cost: Estimated between $70-100 million

Status: Plant design has begun

* * *

Index

Abourezk, Senator James, *xv*
Amerada Hess, 92
American Gas Associates, 74
American Petroleum Institute, *xvi*
Amex Coal, 61
antitrust: and anticompetitive behavior, 98; Horizontal Divestiture Bill, 95; and public policy, 4; and substitutability, 45
Arch Mineral Corp., 43
Arco: uranium, 15
Ashland Oil, 43
asymmetry: concept of, 90

Baeder, Donald, 83
Bain, Joe, 23; atomistic market structure, 10; on collusion, 20
Bankers Trust Co., 47
barrier to entry: analysis of capital outlay, 56; asymmetry, 90; and concentration, 2; Horizontal Divestiture Bill, 95; patents, licensing, 76
Bayh, Senator Birch, *xv*
Bureau of the Mines, 74

capital: availability for electric utilities, 59; and corporate debt, 57; for energy expansion, 46; investment, 28; resources of oil companies, *xxi*, 63
Cities Service Co., 92
coal, *xvi*; analysis in Duchesneau, 9; capital outlay analysis, 48-53; concentration and production, 14; Conoco, 41; consumption, 100; independent producers, 61; pricing and marketplace, 136; producers, *xx*; R&D, 77, 78; R&D history, 83; reserves, *xx*; and residual oil, 33; transportation options, 38, 39
collusion: asymmetry, 90; concentration ratio and likelihood of, 20; and conscious parallelism, 1; and level of concentration, 91; unlikelihood, 98
competition, *xvi*; asymmetry and collusion, 94; and barriers to entry, 2; and coal pricing, 37; collusion, 89; interfuel, 31; and joint ventures, 21; and public policy, 30
Concentrated Industries Act, 4
concentration: and government ownership of energy reserves, 20; horizontal divestiture, 23; impact, 7; level, 97; market structure, 11; and profit-maximization, in Bain, 3; ratio and competition, 2; in Schumpeter, 67; trends, 16; in uranium, 15
conscious parallelism, *xxi*, 1
Consolidation Coal, 45; R&D, 77
consumption: and need for diversification, 100; profit-maximization behavior, 101; rate, *xix*
Continental (Conoco), 17, 36, 41, 45; reserves, 20, 41; uranium, 15

development: capital and risk, 59; cost of R&D innovation, 66; demonstration processes, 74; and diversification, 17; and patents, 70

diversification: assymmetry, 28
divestiture: impact, 85; Interfuel Competition Act, *xv*; social gains, 104
Duchesneau, T.D., 9

Eastern Fuel and Gas Associates, 61
electricity, 31; electric utility industry, 59
Elzinga, K. and Hogarty, T., 9
energy, *xvi*; alternate and horizontal diversification, 99; capital needs, 60; capital outlay analysis, 48-53; capital requirements, 46, 47; concentration trends, 12; entry and profitability, 76; industry defined, 8; possibility of collusion, 93; resources of petroleum firms, 64
environment, 39
Environmental Protection Agency, 35
ERDA, 74
ESECA (Energy Supply and Environmental Coordination Act), 35
exports: historical, *xix*
Exxon, 17, 93; coal R&D, 84; pricing strategy, 36; uranium, 15

FEA (Federal Energy Administration), 35; coal predictions, 61
Federal Trade Commission, *xv*; *Concentration Levels and Trends . . .*, 23; interfuel substitutability, 8, 33
Federal Trade Commission v. Exxon et al., *xv*
Friedman, Benjamin M., 53

Getty Oil Co., 17, 92; reserves, 20; uranium, 15
Goldston, Eli, 61
Gordon, R.L., 45
Gulf, 92; Pittsburgh and Midway Coal Co., 44

Harris, Fred, *xvi*
Hart, Senator Philip, *xv*, *xvi*
Hogan, William, 59
Hogarty, T., 9
horizontal diversification: and asymmetry in petroleum industry, 91; concept of, 10; diversification impact, 89; and joint ventures, 22; Scherer, 23
Horizontal Divestiture Bill, 94
Hunt, Michael, 90

Industrial Reorganization Act, 5
Island Creek Coal Co., 43
Institute of Gas Technology, 74

Interfuel Competition Act, *xv, xvii, xxi*, 101; concentrations, *xxii*; concept of national energy market, 8; and development, 17; Owen Johnson, 24
interfuel substitutability: concept of, 7
investment: analysis of capital outlay, 55; attractions and risk, 58; nonpetroleum energy, *xxi*

Johnson, Owen, 17, 24

Kauper, Thomas E., 21, 23
Kaysen, Carl, 3
Kennecott, 17, 60
Kennedy, Edward, 27; petroleum industry behavior, 79
Kerr-McGee, 85
Kiewit, Peter, 61

legislation, *xvi*; and joint ventures, 22
licensing: commercialization and revenues, 75; cycle of R&D, 72; and technology transfer, 28, 77

management: expertise and oil companies, *xxi*; risk, 30
marketplace: analysis of capital outlay, 50-54; and resource reallocation, *xxi*; trends, 12
market power, 2; concept of, 4, 5; pricing and manipulation, 98
market structure: and capital investments, 65
Measday, Walter, *xvi*
methodology: questionnaires, interviews, 29, 30
mining: profile, 59, 60
Mobil, 92
monopoly, *xxi*; tendencies, in Bain, 3

natural gas, *xvi*; concentration and production, 13; market analysis, 9
Neal, Phil C., 4
North American Coal, 61
NSF, 74
nuclear power: consumption, 100; electrical power generation, 47; Kerr-McGee, 85; producers, *xx*; technology of, *xx*

Occidental Petroleum Co., 43, 93; oil shale, 83
Old Ben Coal Co., 44
oligopolistic behavior, 1; oligopoly defined, 4

Packwood, Senator Bob, *xv*
patent: coal conversion, 73; overview, 70
Peabody Coal, 60
petroleum industry: asymmetry, 91; capital outlay analysis, 48-53; and coal pricing, 36; and concept of total energy companies, *xx*; definition of "industry," 7; Edward Kennedy, 27; multi-energy resources, 78; profile, 62
Petroleum Industry Competition Act, 24
Phillips, 92
pipelines, 39
Pittston, 61
pricing, 28; price parallelism, 33; utilities and multisource energy, 32
production: artificial constraints, 28; asymmetry in reserves, 23; consumption gap, *xix*; and reserve potential, 18; steelmakers and mining companies, 59
Project Independence, *xvii, xix*
public policy: asymmetry, 90; concentration levels, 23; concentration ratios, 11; and firm concentration, *xxii*; firm size and R&D intensity, 65; historical, *xix*; Horizontal Divestiture Bill, 95; and Project Independence, *xx*; social costs of divestiture, 104; and uranium trends, 15

research and development (R&D), *xvi*, 28; and capital investments, 65; Conoco, 83; focus, 78; intensity and analysis, 69; patents and output, 70; petroleum companies, *xx*; pollution controls, 79; profitability, 76; in Schumpeter, 67; trends, 81
reserves: asymmetry, 23; concentration ratio and industry analysis, 11; Kerr-McGee, 85; and resource allocation, *xix, xx*

resource allocation: energy, 47; R&D trends, 81
Rockefeller, Nelson, *xx*

Scherer, 68
Schumpeter, Joseph, 66
Schwartzman, David, 33
Shell Oil, 17
Singer, Eugene, 2
Sohio: Old Ben Coal, 44; and reserves, 20
Standard of California, 17
Standard of Indiana, 20
steelmakers: profile, 59, 60
Sun Oil Co.: coal R&D, 84

technology: capital outlay analysis, 48-53; competence, 85; energy economy, *xx*; energy resource investment, 58; and interfuel substitutability, 8; licensing, 72; R&D trends, 81; switching fuel source, 35; transfer to non-oil energy, *xxi*; transfer and R&D, 77
Texaco, 17, 93; coal R&D, 84
transportation: and coal industry, 9; as factor in coal pricing, 38, 39
treasury Department, *xvi*
Tunney, Senator John, *xv*
Turner, Donald, 3

Union Oil, 92; geothermal energy, 84; oil shale, 83
uranium, *xvi*; concentration and production, 14; Kerr-McGee, 85
utilities: electric, 59; fuel substitutability, 33; and interfuel substitutability, 8; marketplace, 30; switching fuel source, 35

vertical integration: concept of, 10

Westmoreland Coal, 61
White House Task Force on Antitrust Policy, 4
withholding of production: concept of, 97, 98

About the Authors

Jesse W. Markham is an economist. His professional interests in public policy toward business are reflected in this study of the effects of divestiture on the petroleum industry in particular, and on the energy industries in general. His previous publications include *Competition in the Rayon Industry*, *The Fertilizer Industry: Study of An Imperfect Market*, *The American Economy*, and *Conglomerate Enterprise and Public Policy*, as well as contributions to *The American Economic Review*, *The Journal of Political Economy*, *The Southern Economic Journal*, *The Saturday Review of Literature*, and numerous law journals. He has taught economics and public policy at Vanderbilt University, Princeton University, and Harvard University. He also served for two years as Director of the Bureau of Economics of the Federal Trade Commission. He is presently the Charles Edward Wilson Professor of Business Administration at the Harvard Business School and a Faculty Principal with Management Analysis Center, Inc.

Anthony P. Hourihan is a business economist currently finishing his Ph.D. in Business Economics at Harvard Business School where he taught as an instructor in the M.B.A. program during the period 1974-1976. His previous training was in Marketing and his research interests are in economics, finance, marketing, and general business administration. He will be rejoining the HBS faculty in the fall of 1977 to teach in the Finance Area.

Francis L. Sterling is a Vice President of Management Analysis Center, Inc., an international management consulting firm. He received his undergraduate degree in Engineering from the Polytechnic Institute of Brooklyn and an M.B.A. from the University of Pennsylvania's Wharton School of Finance and Commerce. He has been a consultant to many domestic and foreign organizations, such as Canada's Department of Industry, Trade and Commerce, the Industrial Mining and Development Bank of Iran, Sperry Rand and General Electric specializing in market and financial analysis and strategic planning.

FALVEY MEMO
VI